3/10

Personality and the Fate
of Organizations

Pg119ff Demiles

Personality and the Fate of Organizations

Robert Hogan
Hogan Assessment Systems, Inc.

Psychology Press
Taylor & Francis Group

New York   London

Lawrence Erlbaum Associates, Inc., Publishers
10 Industrial Avenue
Mahwah, New Jersey 07430
www.erlbaum.com

Cover art by Harvey Sibley

Library of Congress Cataloging-in-Publication Data

Hogan, Robert, 1937–
Personality and the fate of organizations / Robert Hogan.
p. cm.
Includes bibliographical references and index.
ISBN 0-8058-4142-3 (cloth : alk. paper)
ISBN 0-8058-4143-1 (pbk. : alk. paper)
ISBN 1-4106-1499-9 (e-book)
1. Organizational behavior. 2. Personality. 3. Management—Psych-
ological aspects. 4. Organizational effectiveness.   I. Title.

HD58.7.H642   2006
302.3'5—dc22   2006010473
                                                  CIP

Books published by Lawrence Erlbaum Associates are printed on acid-
free paper, and their bindings are chosen for strength and durability.

Printed in the United States of America
10 9 8 7 6 5 4 3

Contents

Preface   vii

1 What Is Personality Psychology? Defining   1
the Key Issues and Concepts

2 The Personality Wars: A Brief History of Modern   16
Personality Psychology

3 Who Shall Rule? Leadership and Personality   31

4 Lives in Public: Personality and Team Performance   52

5 The Secret Life of Organizations: Personality   80
and Organizational Theory

6 The Psychology of Managerial Incompetence   101

7 How to Fix Incompetence   134

References   152

Author Index   161

Subject Index   165

Figures

4.1 Metatheoretical model of team effectiveness   62

4.2 The Holland model of vocational types   70

Tables

4.1 Belbin's Taxonomy of Team Roles   66

4.2 Task Classification   68

6.1 Why U.S. Presidents Fail   113

6.2 Comparative Results of Three Studies of Managerial 116
         Derailment

6.3 Standard Personality Disorders   118

6.4 Strengths and Shortcomings of the Derailment Factors 132

7.1 The Domain Model   141

Preface

One individual can change the destiny of a nation.

—Old Buddhist proverb

Three considerations prompted me to write this volume. They reflect my concerns about (a) the way psychologists think about the nature and utility of the concept of personality, (b) the way they think about leadership and managerial competence, and (c) the way they think about people in organizations. I believe that these topics are largely misunderstood; certainly, my views on these subjects depart substantially from the received opinion of mainstream psychology. Moreover, the topics are related, because leadership and managerial performance are a direct function of a person's personality, and, in turn, they directly influence the effectiveness of organizations. The confusion has come about in two ways. First, at least until recently, psychologists doubted the relevance—perhaps even the existence—of personality, and therefore the utility of personality assessment.

Second, since the late 1920s, applied psychology has been ideologically predisposed to support management practices, as opposed to being sympathetic with labor issues (Kornhauser, 1930; Zickar, 2001). The first department of applied psychology in the United States, at Carnegie Tech in Pittsburgh, was closed in 1923 precisely because the faculty were involved in labor reform and worked with Samuel Gompers, the president of the biggest steelworkers' union at the time. Thus, industrial/organizational (I/O) psychology has historically been pro-management. Consistent with this pro-management bias, business psychologists typically overestimate the competence of managers across the spectrum of organizations in which people work. This volume is about using personality to understand, evaluate, select, deselect, and train managers; to staff teams; and to understand organizations.

The book strives to be nontechnical and hopefully will interest anyone who is curious about people, careers, and organizational politics. At the same time, the volume is largely empirical, so that the major statements and claims are mostly supported by evidence. Many smart nonpsychologists who have read and commented on draft chapters have claimed to find them interesting and intelligible.

The book begins with an introduction to and overview of personality theory. Although personality theory is about human nature and should be of great general interest, it is not a prominent feature of the undergraduate psychology curriculum and few readers will have a background in the subject. Thus, this introduction seems necessary. Chapter 2 is a brief intellectual history of personality psychology over the past 50 years. I try to show why, despite the obvious importance of personality psychology, it nearly went away as a discipline, and why it has recently reemerged. Chapter 3 concerns leadership and personality. I argue that individual differences in the talent for leadership are real, that they are related empirically to personality, and that who a person is determines how that person will lead.

Chapter 4 concerns personality and team performance. Most significant human accomplishments come from group efforts. This chapter shows how group efforts can be reduced to the contributions of individuals. I conclude the chapter with a discussion of the practical problem of team development. Chapter 5 is about organizational theory. I describe certain universal, unavoidable, and recurring themes in organizations that recur precisely because they reflect universal themes in human nature. This chapter is an effort to explain the dynamics of organizations in terms of individual personalities. Chapter 6 returns to the topic of leadership; leadership is the link between individual personality and the performance of organizations. In this chapter, I argue that it is a mistake to confuse leadership with the behavior of business executives, elected public officials, and senior military officers. I argue further that many of these people will fail as leaders, then enumerate the reasons for their failure, all of which are rooted in their personalities. Finally, in chapter 7 I outline methods for improving the performance of existing leaders. When the performance of existing leaders improves, the change will improve the quality of life for their subordinates and the performance of the organizational units for which they are responsible.

The book is unique in two ways. First, it takes personality seriously—it assumes that personality is real, and that it determines the careers of individuals and the fate of organizations. Second, it shows how large-scale organizational phenomena—the subject matter of sociology, history, and political science—can be (and indeed should be) understood in terms of the aspirations and behavior of single individuals—in terms of human nature.

1

What Is Personality Psychology?
Defining the Key Issues and Concepts

Personality psychology concerns the nature of human nature. It answers three general questions: (a) How and in what ways are we all alike; (b) how and in what ways are we all different; and (c) why do we (as individuals) do what we do? Why should anyone be interested in personality psychology? There are three reasons. The first is pragmatic: Because other people are the most consequential, helpful, and dangerous parts of the environment in which we live, it seems sensible to have some understanding of these (often) dark forces. Second, without a theory of some sort, it is difficult to make sense out of the world. All of us have more or less well articulated theories of human nature, but these theories are almost surely in need of some maintenance and even repair. We need to understand personality to make sense of the personal, business, and political worlds in which we live. Third, true change depends on understanding how the world works. If we want to improve our lives, relationships, careers, business organizations, or societies, we need as accurate a view of human nature as we can devise.

This volume has two overarching goals. The first is to present a relatively systematic perspective on personality, based on many years of reading, research, and reflection. The second is to use this perspective to understand managers and business organizations. In my view, the success or failure of organizations, ranging in complexity from the family to the multinational corporation and the modern nation-state, depend crucially on the personalities of the persons in charge of the organizations. In a sense, then, this is a book about organizational theory from a blatantly reductionist perspective—I want to explain the dynamics of organizations in terms of the personalities of the key actors. Most people who work in and try to manage real organizations understand how important it is to have the right person in the right job, and this understanding is a tacit acknowledgment of the significance of personality.

This volume is intended for a literate audience. Although I hope psychologists will find it interesting, I am seeking a more general reader. The work probably falls in the category of a self-help book, but my goal is not to increase or enhance individual self-understanding. Rather, my goal is to increase the reader's ability to understand other people—how they are all alike, how they are all different, and why they do what they do. Armed with this understanding, the reader should then be able to pursue his or her personal, social, and organizational goals more efficiently. This first chapter concerns definitions: I define the key issues in personality psychology, the core assumptions and claims on which the subsequent discussion depends. In the next chapter, I review the modern history of personality psychology—its emergence and early popularity, its rapid subsequent descent into neglect, and its modern renaissance. Chapter 2 is necessary to put the book's key argument—that personality drives leadership, which then drives organizational performance—into context.

ORGANIZING ASSUMPTIONS

I believe in truth in advertising—I believe in alerting others to my key assumptions. My most fundamental assumption is that the methods of science are our most reliable guide to understanding reality. In that context, I think biology and evolutionary theory provide the necessary framework for understanding human nature.

I base my model of personality on four generalizations drawn from the vast and rapidly expanding literature on human origins. The first generalization is that we evolved as group-living animals, which means that we always live in groups, group living is our natural environment, and our natural tendency is to agglutinate. The second generalization is that every group has a status hierarchy. In some groups (e.g., Cistercian monks) the hierarchies may be hard to discern (for the monks, status is determined by individual differences in how strictly the rules of chastity, poverty, and silence are observed), but they are always there. Moreover, the hierarchies begin developing very early and they are quite powerful: A younger colleague complained recently about his 3-year-old daughter's preschool group. Two 5-year-old girls "ruled" the group, and the mothers of the younger girls were pestered, every morning, by their daughters' demands to wear that day what the 5-year-old rulers had worn the day before.

The third generalization is that every human group has a religion of some sort. Not only are religions a cultural universal, but religious observances also seem to be an ancient feature of human groups. Anthropologists have evidence of systematic burial practices 100,000 years ago. Such practices probably go back further, but hard data are difficult to obtain. Nested within the religious practices of each group are vast numbers of prescribed and proscribed behaviors (e.g., husbands should not look at their mother-in-laws, be careful not to allow others to obtain pieces of your fingernails, prepare foods in certain ways, etc.) that we moderns arrogantly deem superstitions, while treasuring our own strange rules and practices.

The final generalization concerns the fact that all hunter-gatherer societies—from tribesmen in the New Guinea highlands to the Inuits in Greenland to the !Kung Bushmen in the Kalahari Desert of South Africa—live in egalitarian bands (Boehm, 1999). Anthropologists mostly agree that existing hunter-gatherer societies (which are rapidly disappearing) are the best model we have for estimating the structure of human society in prehistory. The living conditions of modern hunter-gatherers suggest that egalitarian living arrangements are a natural part of human psychology. Every hunter-gatherer group has a "head man," but they become head men on the basis of (a) their moral qualities—they resolve disputes and generally work to keep the peace; (b) their good judgment—they make good decisions about where to find food, water, and shelter; and (c) their skill as hunters. These head men lead by example, and are rarely able to demand that the rest of the group obey them.

There are two additional points to be noted about hunter-gatherer societies. First, in most of these groups, from time to time, one member (almost always a male) will try to dominate the others (e.g., take extra food, not share his resources, bully others, and take other men's wives). The subsequent history of these efforts to dominate others takes a predictable course. First the group warns the miscreant. If the bullying continues, the group shuns the offender. If the bullying continues, the group may physically isolate the bad boy. Finally, if the misbehavior continues, the group executes the bully, either in an ambush or by setting him up to be taken by a rival group. This suggests that hatred of domination is also part of the innate human cognitive apparatus, a point that has important implications for our later discussion of managerial performance.

My final point based on the study of human origins is that, when the world emerged from the last ice age about 13,000 years ago, all humans lived in hunter-gatherer societies. Agriculture was invented in the east end of the Mediterranean Sea about 11,000 years ago, and this invention brought about a profound change in the structure of human groups (Diamond, 1997). Groups began to stay in one geographical location, individuals began to accumulate resources (the accumulation of resources is *verboten* in egalitarian hunter-gatherer communities), and with resources, individuals with aspirations could recruit and pay others to support their efforts to dominate the local communities. Some time in the last 6,000 years we saw, for the first time, the emergence of the hierarchies, tyrannies, and kleptocracies that characterize the modern world. At the time of the rise of Rome 2,000 years ago, about half the world's population lived in hunter-gatherer bands. The ancient Greeks are typically credited with inventing democracy, but in reality they merely rediscovered the social structure of their prehistorical ancestors. It is fairly easy to see the history of the modern world over the past 2,000 years in terms of the rise of various dictatorships, followed by a series of spontaneous attempts to overthrow these tyrannies and restore a measure of egalitarianism in everyday life.

To summarize the foregoing, I base my analysis of personality on these four generalizations: (a) people always live in groups, (b) every group has a status hierarchy, (c) every group has a religion and an assortment of prescribed and proscribed behaviors, and (d) people are adapted to live in groups that resemble hunter-gatherer societies. These generalizations allow us to draw some inferences about the nature of human motivation; that is, how we are all alike.

MOTIVATION

The fact that people evolved as group-living animals and continue to do so today suggests that, at a deep and perhaps unconscious level, people need social companionship, social feedback, and social interaction. People are preprogrammed to seek the company of others. It also suggests that people will find social isolation quite stressful, and the prospects of being shunned, rejected, and isolated are quite threatening. Data supporting this suggestion are found in Harlow's research regarding the devastating impact of social isolation on baby rhesus monkeys—research so painful as to make it unthinkable to replicate it with human infants. More immediate data are to be found in research on attachment theory (Bowlby, 1969). This research demonstrates that infants find separation from their primary caretakers to be deeply traumatizing. Bowlby, the originator of attachment theory, noted that for a child to be separated from his or her caretakers is like being exposed to radiation: Any amount is harmful and it accumulates. Writers as different as Adam Smith and J. J. Rousseau have argued that humans are inherently social animals. As is the case with any generalization about people, there are individual differences: Some people are powerfully motivated by the prospects of social contact (extroverts), and some people prefer to remain by themselves (introverts). Moreover, there will be important individual differences in peoples' ability to develop and maintain a network of social relationships. Finally, personality psychologists have developed good measures of individual differences in these affiliative desires and capabilities.

The fact that every human (and primate) group is organized in terms of a status hierarchy suggests that, at a deep and perhaps unconscious level, people need status and try to promote and advance their positions in their social groups when they can. It also suggests that people will find the loss of status deeply threatening and traumatic. Consider, for example, the seemingly illogical behavior of Saddam Hussein, the former dictator of Iraq, who by defying the world community risked bringing chaos and destruction to the people of his country. His behavior becomes interpretable and even logical when seen in terms of a powerful desire not to lose the status that he spent his life acquiring. Once again, however, there will be important individual differences in the degree to which people want status, with some people being obsessed with such aspirations and others being relatively indifferent to worldly rank. Among those who want to advance themselves, there will be important individual differences in abilities to do so. Finally, personality psychologists have developed good measures of individual differences in these desires and capabilities for status attainment.

The fact that every human culture has a religion and an associated network of rules designed to regulate conduct suggests that, at a deep and perhaps unconscious level, people need structure, order, predictability, and even meaning in their lives. People create myths, legends, religious systems, and moralities to provide themselves with structure, predictability, and meaning. There is a very interesting but somewhat overlooked literature on the experimental induction of neurosis in laboratory animals; this literature clearly demonstrates these needs in rats and dogs. In the first such experiment, Pavlov, the Nobel prize-winning Russian physiologist, strapped a dog in a harness, then required the dog to distinguish between a circle and an ellipse. If the dog correctly chose the circle, it received a meat powder; if it chose the ellipse, it received nothing. Pavlov varied the positions of the circle and ellipse, and made each ellipse closer to a circle. At some point, the dog experienced a severe nervous breakdown simply by being required to make choices in an increasingly ambiguous situation. Chimpanzees also become highly emotional when confronted with strange and ambiguous circumstances. As is always the case, there are important individual differences in the degree to which people can tolerate ambiguity and uncertainty, and personality psychologists have developed good measures of peoples' ability to tolerate risk and uncertainty.

I end this discussion of motivation with three observations. First, there are other motives at play in everyday life. For example, we share with reptiles the needs for food, water, territory, sex, and the desire to protect our young. We share with chimpanzees the needs for social contact and status. The motivational model I have described here is, I believe, distinctly human. Second, the needs for social contact, status, and structure are principally resolved during social interaction. In an important sense, humans are compelled to interact, we are most distinctly human and ourselves during social interaction, and outside of our normal patterns of interaction, we have little to do except surf the Internet. Finally, I use as shorthand terms for these three motive patterns the phrases *getting along, getting ahead,* and *making meaning.* Our needs for acceptance and social contact lead to behaviors designed to get along; our needs for status result in behaviors designed to get ahead; and our needs for predictability and order lead to behaviors designed to make meaning.

SOCIAL INTERACTION

All consequential human action takes place during social interaction. What we do in private, to a substantial degree, consists of reviewing past interactions and planning for future interactions. It is useful to reflect for a moment on the ingredients of interactions. All interactions have three essential components. The first is an agenda, a reason for the interaction. Agendas range from the trivial and informal ("Let's get together and have a beer") to the profound and formal (United Nations Security Council debates). Persons with power or social skill are often able to set the agenda for interactions. The second necessary component for an interaction is roles to play: We can only interact with others in the context of roles, which provide needed structure and predictability. Consider the children's game of jump rope: The game can only take place if there is some agreement about playing the game, and if there are enough children to fill the required roles of rope turner and rope jumper. Roles range from informal (guest at a cocktail party) to formal (bride in a wedding ceremony). There are important individual differences in peoples' abilities to define and play roles, and skillful players generally do better in the game of life.

The final ingredient needed for interactions is the rules for the game, ritual, or ceremony in which a person is involved. These rules are usually well understood by the participants prior to the interaction, although they are often subject to negotiation (e.g., the rules governing professional football games are periodically revised to enhance the crowd appeal of the games). The socialization process, which begins in infancy and continues thereafter, is largely about teaching people the requirements of various roles, and the rules that apply in various kinds of interaction. People who do not honor the requirements of their roles or who ignore the rules for the interaction put the integrity of the game at risk and are often asked to leave the interaction. Consider the formal interactions known as college lectures. The major agenda concerns students learning something from a lecturer. Persons in the role of the lecturer are supposed to look a certain way and be prepared to lecture; persons in the role of student are supposed to pretend to care about the lecture. Even small deviations from the norms (e.g., a male instructor wearing a red evening gown, a student talking quietly on a cell phone) will threaten to disrupt the proceedings. Again, this speaks to our needs for structure, predictability, and order, and how we invent rituals to meet these needs.

PERSONALITY

In everyday language the word *personality* has two meanings. These meanings serve very different purposes, and for the sake of rational conversation, it is important to keep the two meanings distinct. On the one hand, there is the actor's view of personality; this is personality from the inside and it concerns the you that you know—the person you think you are; your hopes, dreams, aspirations, values, fears, and theories about how to get along, get ahead, and find meaning (McAdams, 1993). On the other hand, there is the observer's view of personality; this is personality from the outside and it concerns the you that we know—the person others think you are, based on your overt behavior.

There are several important points to be noted about these two aspects of personality. First, we refer to the actor's view of personality as your *identity,* whereas the the observer's view of personality is referred to as your *reputation.* Your identity is the story you tell yourself and others about you; it is the generic part that you play during social interaction. Your reputation is the summary evaluation of your past performances during interaction as shared by the members of your community. Second, the concepts of identity and reputation serve very different functions in everyday language. We use reputation to describe your past performances or to predict your future performance—reputations are used to describe or predict behavior. We use identity to explain your behavior. Reputation concerns what you do, and identity concerns why you do it.

Thoughtful nonpsychologists have always understood the point of distinguishing between personality from the inside and from the outside. For example, consider the following comments in a 2003 issue of *The New York Times Review of Books* regarding Browne's (2002) magnificent biography of Darwin:

> So, after a thousand pages, do we know the man? ... Browne ... speculates very little about [Darwin's] interior life. There are few cases, probably, in which we can know much about a person's inner being—biographers who purport to know about such matters are usually impertinent or fanciful or both .... Still, Browne gives us a vivid sense of what

can be legitimately described: how he appeared to his family, his friends, and the public at large. (p. 31)

The point is that we can talk with knowledge about reputation, but our observations about another person's identity are typically speculative at best.

A third point to remember about identity and reputation concerns their relative degrees of verifiability or truth value. Identity, once again, concerns the you that you know. Sigmund Freud, the Viennese psychiatrist and founder of psychoanalysis, would say that the you that you know is hardly worth knowing. This is because we invent ourselves; our identity is a story that we made up to give us a part to play in social interaction. It is empirically well established that peoples' self-stories are only tangentially related to their past performances, and in many cases are radically discrepant with them. Identities are quite hard to study in a rigorous fashion largely because they are so subjective and even fanciful. In contrast, reputation is easy to study: We simply ask the peer community to describe an actor using a standardized reporting format. Such descriptions typically show a high degree of agreement across the persons who provide them, and such descriptions tend to be very stable over long periods of time. Moreover, because the best predictor of future behavior is past behavior, and because reputations reflect past behavior, reputations are the best single predictors of a person's future behavior. Finally, extensive research over the past 100 years shows that there is a very stable and even universal structure to reputations. Regardless of the culture in which a person lives, or the language that his or her peer community speaks, all reputations can be characterized in terms of five broad themes (self-confidence, extroversion, agreeableness, conscientiousness, and curiosity). Personality psychologists refer to this finding as the Five-Factor Model (FFM; Wiggins, 1996). The development of the FFM has had a profound affect on personality research since about 1990.

Finally, no matter how fanciful or contrived a person's identity may be, it is the core and bedrock of each person's psychological being, and the primary means by which each person guides and interprets his or her life. This fact leads to an interesting paradox. Although actors are primarily concerned about their identities, observers are more concerned about the actors' reputations. Affection and status are granted on the basis of reputation—people hire us, fire us, marry us, loan us money, and otherwise support us based on our reputations. Consequently, smart players will reverse the natural order of their thinking and pay close attention to how others perceive and evaluate them.

DEVELOPMENT

Personality development concerns how we get to be the persons we are. Consistent with my interest in biology, I subscribe to the (very well supported) notion that a good bit (perhaps 50%) of personality is genetic and laid down at birth. That which is laid down at birth is *temperament.* Temperament is the foundation on which the house of personality is built, and it is manifested in certain relatively well-defined behavioral tendencies and certain pervasive and well-defined mood states. The behavioral components of temperament vary along three dimensions. The first is sociability—some babies are naturally cuddly and enjoy contact with strangers, whereas others are shy and dislike meeting strangers. The second behavioral component of temperament is emotionality—some babies are easily upset and hard to soothe, whereas others are rarely upset and easy to soothe. The third component is impulsivity—some babies are fearless and quick to act, whereas others are cautious and slow to act.

There are three well-studied components of mood that seem genetic in origin and closely parallel the behavioral components of temperament. The first, *positive affectivity,* is defined by characteristically sunny, cheerful, and upbeat mood states. The second, *negative affectivity,* is defined by characteristically dysphoric mood states. The third is called *restraint,* and is defined by caution and apparent timidity. Temperament is probably the most stable part of personality: It affects how we interpret experience and therefore construct our identities, and it affects our behavior and how others construct our reputations. Strictly speaking, however, temperament is not part of development; it is a precursor to development.

I believe that personality development can be conceptualized in terms of four stages or periods. Each stage is defined by a particular developmental problem or challenge, and how each of these is resolved has consequences for personality in adulthood. I believe these stages are universal, so that people everywhere must move through them. They are as follows:

1. *Infancy.* Infancy extends from birth until the time when a child joins the children's play group, around 4 or 5 years. During this first

stage, children are primarily concerned with adapting to the demands of their parents. The degree to which the parents provide an appropriate degree of warmth and affection and set appropriate limits for a child's behavior will affect two broad aspects of personality: core self-esteem and attitudes toward authority. Core self-esteem impacts a person's ability to deal with adversity, whereas attitudes toward authority influence a person's self-control and willingness to follow rules. Attitudes toward authority translate into conscientiousness in adulthood. Personality psychologists have developed very good measures of core self-esteem and conscientiousness, and these measures are very robust predictors of occupational performance in adulthood (Judge, Erez, & Bono, 1998; Ones, Viswesvaran, & Schmidt, 1993). I regard self-esteem and conscientiousness as the key determinants of a person's basic employability. These components of personality develop early and are hard to change in adulthood.

2. *Childhood.* Children are programmed to move into their peer cohort sometime around the fourth or fifth year of life. When they do, the ability of their parents to control and influence them begins steadily to decline, and the power of the peer group begins steadily to increase. The ability to anticipate other's expectations facilitates a child's entrance into and participation in the peer group. Learning to think about one's own behavior from the perspective of the others with whom one interacts is a kind of skill. This skill is the exact opposite of the egocentrism and self-centeredness of small children—and it is a skill that many adults never develop very well. Perspective taking is a disposition or skill that can be, to some degree, trained or developed in later life. Personality psychologists have developed some good measures of perspective taking. Those measures predict important aspects of occupational performance, especially in jobs and tasks that require working as part of a team.

3. *Early adolescence.* During early adolescence, young people begin their transition out of the peer group and into the adult world of work. They also begin the transition away from parental care and control and into a life where they will provide for themselves, take some responsibility for their own lives, and perhaps contribute to society. The major factor involved in this transition is learning how to use the tools and technology of the culture, developing some skills so that they can earn a living. In developed societies, much of this learning takes place in formal training programs; in underdeveloped societies, the learning takes place in the field or on the job. An important re-

lated factor involved in this transition is learning how to live and work with people other than one's parents or peer group. The skills acquired during this phase of development are all learned and can be changed by further learning. The ability to master the technical skills required to transition into adulthood can be assessed reasonably well by measures of cognitive ability (IQ).

4. *Adulthood.* The most important psychological task of adulthood involves developing a story about one's life that makes sense of one's past and paints a picture of the future. It is like developing a vision statement for one's career: This is what I stand for and this is why I stand for it. Another word for this story or personal vision statement is a sense of identity. A sense of identity, the story we tell ourselves about who we are and what we stand for, is also what we mean by personality from the perspective of the actor. The empirical study of identity is relatively new (i.e., McAdams, 1993), it is somewhat tedious to measure identity, and the consequences for careers of various kinds of identity are not well understood. I can report three generalizations with some confidence. First, persons with poorly articulated identities or personal stories do not do very well in terms of their careers. Second, persons with well-articulated identities are seen as mature and wholesome. Finally, because a sense of identity develops relatively late, it is also relatively easy to change, especially compared to the outcomes of first two stages of development.

CHARACTER AND PERSONALITY

When the systematic study of personality first began, the words *personality* and *character* were often used interchangeably. Character is an old-fashioned word, but one that seems to be returning to more common usage, and it refers (as it did for the ancient Greeks) to a certain kind of personality. The model of personality development I just described is also a model of character development. Persons who experience positive results during the first stage of development have positive attitudes toward rules and authority, respect tradition, and are models of probity. Persons who experience a positive outcome during the second stage of development are insightful and respectful of other people's rights and expectations, understand the concept of reciprocity, and have an intuitive sense of justice. The third stage of development is about developing life and career skills, but the fourth stage concerns developing a vision or rationale for one's life and career, a metaphysical justification, as it were. People who can frame their lives in broad moral terms are always rated as morally mature (cf. Hogan, 1973).

Conversely, people who hate rules and authority, people who are insensitive to social expectations and indifferent to questions of justice, and people who are unable to describe their moral vision, or those who endorse a blighted vision, are perceived as wicked, and indeed behave wickedly (Hogan, 1973).

THE UNCONSCIOUS

Professionals who practice counseling and psychotherapy all recognize that their clients do things for reasons they do not understand. That is an empirical data point. The existentialist philosophers talk about the universality of self-deception, and the Marxists used to talk about false consciousness. The point is that thoughtful observers of human conduct, both ancient and modern, have noted the tendency for people to give reasons for their actions that seemed sincere but to outside observers seemed wrong or even delusional. The question is how we can account for this phenomenon.

The notion that there are thoughts, memories, desires, and emotions buried deep inside us that control our actions is one of the most titillating ideas in personality psychology. The general concept is at least as old as Plato, and was a prominent part of European philosophy in the 19th century; it was particularly important in the ideas of Hegel, Schopenhauer, and Nietzsche. The concept of the unconscious entered personality psychology in the writings of Freud and Jung. Freud and Jung argued that most of what we do is governed by unconscious impulses, that consciousness and rationality serve the unconscious—they primarily exist to legitimize the promptings of the unconscious. They further argued that neurotic and even psychotic symptoms are caused by a failure to explore and understand the unconscious, and the process of psychoanalysis is designed to do precisely that. The recent spate of interest in recovered memories in the women's movement is a version of the same topic.

As intriguing as Hollywood writers may find this concept of the unconscious, it has some logical problems and it lacks empirical support. The logical problems concern how the thoughts and emotions that now control our behavior became unconscious in the first place. The empirical problem concerns our inability to measure or assess individual differences in the susceptibility to unconscious promptings.

There is, however, an alternative way to think about the unconscious that was nicely captured in an aphorism by Oklahoma humorist Will Rogers, who once famously noted that "It isn't what you don't know that will hurt you, it is what you do know that isn't true." All of us, at least some of the time, base our actions on beliefs that are factually false. For example, narcissists believe they are more competent, attractive, and powerful than do the other people who work with them; their grandiosity and accompanying sense of entitlement inevitably create problems for them in terms of relationship and career development (cf. Hogan & Hogan, 2001).

Experimental psychologists now largely agree that much, if not most, of our everyday life is guided by a set of pervasive unconscious mental processes that we use to understand others, frame goals, set priorities, and evaluate ourselves (Wilson, 2002). However, this is a very different view of the unconscious than the vastly influential views of Freud and Jung. This modern view differs from the views of Freud and Jung in three important ways. First, the modern unconscious is adaptive rather than maladaptive—it helps us navigate everyday life and does not cause mental illness if it is ignored. Second, much of it is learned and can be modified under the proper circumstances, as opposed to being inherited and implacable. Third, the modern unconscious can be explored, investigated, and expressed in relatively straightforward and commonsensical ways—and this view contrasts dramatically with the views of Freud and Jung.

PERSONALITY CHANGE

Personality psychology is defined by the assumption that there are, inside us, some stable and enduring structures that give form and coherence to our behavior and our lives. These stable structures are our personalities, they are what define us and give us our unique qualities. The various writers in the history of personality psychology all agree with this assumption. They differ among themselves only in terms of how they define the structures; they all agree about the reality of the structures and their role in explaining our behavior.

Not all psychologists agree with this assumption, of course. The powerful and influential group of writers who adopt a behaviorist orientation (e.g., Mischel, 1968) flatly disagree with the assumption of stable structures. They argue that (a) there is little evidence to support the assumption, and (b) what people do is determined by their situations and circumstances, rather than by imaginary stable structures. I often wonder how these behaviorists are able to write letters of recommendation; that is, the logic of their argument dictates that they can only say, "Mr. Jones will be a high performer in the right circumstances and a poor performer in the wrong circumstances."

Nonetheless, one of the most persistent and long-standing objections to traditional personality psychology concerns the issue of change. Can people change? If they can change, how much can they change? American society, with its commitment to democratic values, has always believed in the possibility of personal change, growth, and redemption, and that in part explains the enduring appeal of behaviorist thinking: People are attracted to the view that, if people are placed in different circumstances, they will be different and possibly better. Personality, with its commitment to the notion of stable internal structures, seems antidemocratic at its core.

I believe that the question "Can personality change?" can be answered pretty quickly and easily once we have defined personality adequately. If you recall the distinction between identity and reputation (i.e., the distinction between personality from the inside and personality from the outside), the question about change should be framed as three questions. The first is, "Can people change their behavior?" The answer to this is usually, if they really want to. The second question is, "Can people change their identities?" The answer is, people often change the way they think about themselves, sometimes for the better and sometimes not. This, of course, is what psychotherapy is all about. The third question is, "Can people change their reputations?" The answer is, it is very hard to change others' perceptions. As Marshall Goldman, the king of executive coaching says, people have to change their behavior 100% to get a 10% change in how others perceive them. The key to the change process is a change in behavior. If we behave differently, we will begin to perceive ourselves differently, and in time, others will, too.

2

The Personality Wars:
A Brief History
of Modern Personality Psychology

Personality psychology is a powerful and indispensable tool for interpreting and navigating the social world around us. Ideas have consequences—how we think about other people strongly influences how we conduct our lives, at home and at work. Consider two examples from my business experience, and I can multiply these examples almost endlessly. First, I consult with a large trucking company in the southeastern United States that supplies logistics services to two automobile manufacturers, one in Spartanburg, South Carolina, and the other in Jaynesville, Wisconsin. In each location, half of the employees work for the company, and the other employees work for a labor leasing organization. All of the company employees were hired using an integrity measure contained in the Hogan Personality Inventory (HPI; Hogan & Hogan, 1995); none of the leasing company employees had been screened with a personality measure. The employees work side by side, doing the same job, for the same salary, and are directed by the same supervisors. The leased employees have four times as many accidents as the prescreened employees.

This differential accident rate is a commentary on the power of personality versus the power of situational influences. By this I mean that there are really only two ways to explain human behavior: in terms of factors inside people and factors outside people. The factors inside people that influence behavior (genes, interpersonal strategies, traits) are summarized by the term *personality;* the factors outside people (history, culture, the environment) are summarized by the term *situational influences.* Over the years, the advocates of situational influences have been the most strident and persistent critics of personality psychology, and have also persistently ignored evidence such as this.

Second, a few years ago I visited a large East Coast prison; I asked the warden to describe the most important characteristics of a good correctional officer. The warden was a very smart and seasoned professional (and a former professional hockey player). He said that the most crucial skill a prison guard could have was the ability to read the prisoner's personality. Both the officer's safety and the operation of the prison depended on an ability that many psychologists tell us does not exist (cf. Funder, 1987).

When money is on the table or when lives are at stake, normal people understand the importance of personality. Nonetheless, some time in the mid-1960's personality psychology suffered a major crisis of credibility in academic psychology and then virtually disappeared from the intellectual radar. Anyone who studied psychology in the 1970s or 1980s would have been told that there is no such thing as personality, and that personality assessment does not work. Personality psychology has experienced a major and dramatic rebirth—even a renaissance—since the 1990s. The purpose of this chapter is to review the decline, fall, and rebirth of personality psychology over the past 45 years. It is important to review this history because the original critics are determined and energetic, they are still around, and they are still not persuaded of the importance of personality (cf. Schmitt, 2004). Moreover, I encounter their criticisms every day in my efforts to use personality psychology to solve problems in organizations. Veterans of the personality wars should find this history interesting; nonpartisans, however, might even want to skip this chapter.

There are three pretty clear reasons for the near demise of personality psychology in the 1960s. The first two concern self-inflicted wounds, and the third reflects the *weltanschaung* of academic psychology itself.

SELF-INFLICTED WOUND NUMBER 1

The first self-inflicted wound concerns the fact that personality psychologists have never been able to agree about an agenda for their discipline. Personality psychology begins with European (and especially German) psychiatry at the turn of the 20th century. The great European names in the history of the discipline—Freud, Jung, Adler, Horney, Erikson—all assumed that, because childhood seems inevitably traumatic, everyone is more or less neurotic. They concluded, then, that the primary intellectual task of personality psychology is to explain how and why people become neurotic. From this perspective, the practical agenda of personality psychology is to help people overcome their neuroses.

Personality psychology began in the 1930s in the United States as a reaction to this European tradition. The great American names in the history of the discipline—Allport, Murray, Maslow, Rogers—assumed that everyone is motivated by needs for personal growth and self-enhancement, but that these needs are often frustrated. They concluded that the goal of personality psychology is to appreciate how each person has uniquely adapted to the demands of the self-actualization process. The practical agenda of the American tradition is to unblock peoples' natural tendencies to growth and help them self-actualize and become all that they can be.

The third major tradition in personality psychology is represented by a group of mathematically talented English and American men (e.g., Thurstone, Guilford, Cattell, Eysenck, and their students). These men argued that the appropriate agenda for personality psychology is to determine the true underlying structure of personality, which they thought should be defined in terms of a set of statistical abstractions called *traits.* Their research involves developing and administering various personality measures, and then analyzing the statistical relations among the responses. These men had a basic science agenda with no particular practical goal or outcome in mind.

My point, once again, is that, historically, the discipline of personality psychology has never agreed on its intellectual agenda. Moreover, the various agendas that have been proposed have only limited practical consequences. For example, consider the European perspective: What do you know about a person if you know that he or she is not neurotic? You do not know if that person has a sense of humor, integrity, creativity, or talent for leadership. More important, classic research from the Institute of Personality Assessment and Research at Berkeley shows that highly successful and creative people are typically plagued by self-doubt and insecurity (Barron, 1965). In my research with entrepreneurs and successful salespeople, I find that, almost without exception, they have strong needs to demonstrate their personal worth through their accomplishments (cf. Hogan & Hogan, 1991). The absence of neuroticism is not very informative and the presence of neuroticism can be associated with high-level accomplishment. This suggests that the European tradition, despite its historical importance, may have been studying something that does not matter a great deal.

Consider now the traditional American focus on self-actualization and individual uniqueness. What do you do with individual uniqueness after you have described it? By definition, you cannot generalize uniqueness. It follows, then, that the study of individual uniqueness has few practical applications or implications. The third major tradition in personality psychology concerns a search for the underlying statistical structure of personality; this tradition is explicitly other-worldly—by design, it has few practical applications or implications. The first self-inflicted wound of personality psychology concerns the fact that traditional personality psychology lacks any consensus regarding its intellectual agenda, and that its major subdivisions have limited practical implications. Smart people everywhere noticed this incoherence and this has affected their judgment of the utility of personality psychology.

SELF-INFLECTED WOUND NUMBER 2

The second wound that personality psychology inflicted on itself concerns personality assessment. Personality assessment is the core research methodology for personality psychology. Many organizations also use personality assessment to understand people's capabilities and limitations before hiring them or assigning them to training or treatment programs. Sometimes they use assessment results to give people feedback to encourage self-knowledge and self-development. Well-developed assessment procedures are quite helpful—they can be used to predict occupational performance in virtually any job, or to predict training performance in virtually any curriculum (cf. Hogan, 2005). The bad news, however, is that the vast majority of commercially available assessment procedures today are poorly developed and the information they provide is dubious (Paul, 2004). Professional training is required to distinguish between a competent assessment procedure and a fraud.

Personality assessment is a highly evolved technology. It was first developed in the Netherlands in the late 19th century and then spread to the rest of Europe. In the United States, personality assessment was first used during World War I. Army psychologists devised checklists to evaluate draftees' fitness for duty. The items on these checklists concerned overt or obvious symptoms of psychopathology (e.g., anxiety, depression, and delusional thinking). Longer commercial versions of these measures were published in the 1920s and 1930s, including the Bernreuter (1933) and the Minnesota Multiphasic Personality Inventory (MMPI; Butcher, Dahlstrom, Graham, Tellegen, & Kaemmer, 1989).

The development and use of personality measures expanded rapidly after World War II, and exploded with the advent of the computer age. Although most of the new tests and measures were designed to assess aspects of psychopathology, a few (far-sighted) researchers developed personality inventories designed to measure normal personality. These researchers had concluded that measures of psychopathology were not very useful for predicting competence and effectiveness. One of the very best of these new measures of normal personality was the California Psychological Inventory (CPI; Gough, 1954). The CPI was unusual at the time because it was explicitly designed to predict high-level performance rather than neuroticism and mental illness.

In the 1950s and 1960s a large research literature grew up around these new measures. This literature was quite informative in places— for example, research at the University of California at Berkeley definitively identified the personality correlates of creativity (Barron, 1965). However, there was also a lot of confusion, reflecting the fact that anyone can develop a personality measure by writing some items (e.g., "I prefer a shower to a tub bath") and calling the items a test. Unfortunately, professional psychology has no oversight boards responsible for monitoring the technical quality of commercially available tests.

It is important to remember that the definition of an academic is someone who thinks otherwise. No matter how much consensus there might be on any topic or issue, there will always be some respected academics who take passionate exception to that consensus; Freud referred to this as the narcissism of minor differences. In the late 1950s, a small group of statistically minded psychologists began to argue that there was a deep and profound methodological problem at the heart of traditional personality assessment.

These researchers studied the MMPI (Butcher et al., 1989), the gold standard inventory designed to aid psychiatric diagnosis. The researchers rated each item on the MMPI for social desirability (the degree to which an endorsement of that item would be a socially desirable—or undesirable—admission). They then calculated correlations between the social desirability rating of each item and the frequency with which that item was endorsed in the general population, and they found very substantial correlations between rated social desirability and endorsement frequency. They then argued that, when people respond to items on the MMPI (and by extension any other personality inventory), they are not responding to the content of the item (e.g., "I often have strange and unusual thoughts"—an item from the Schizophrenia scale of the MMPI). Rather they are responding to the perceived social desirability of the item. Thus, they argued, all existing measures of personality concern the same thing: They measure social desirability, not personality. According to this argument, there is a damaging statistical artifact at the heart of personality assessment.

The issues raised by the social desirability argument have never been resolved to the satisfaction of the critics of personality assessment. The argument is most visible today in the form of the faking issue—the claim that personality assessments are useless because they are easily faked. The social desirability argument flared for 15 years; it consumed the best minds of the discipline, and it led external observers to conclude that the empirical base of personality psychology was fundamentally flawed. There were two major consequences of this controversy: (a) government funding for personality research dried up, and (b) it became almost impossible to publish assessment-based personality research in academic journals. With no funding and no access to journals, personality psychologists were professionally doomed.

My view is that the entire controversy was beside the point. From a pragmatic perspective, the fundamental issue when evaluating personality assessment is the degree to which scores on an assessment device predict (or are correlated with) relevant behavioral outcomes. For example, if low scores on a measure of integrity predict theft, absenteeism, substance abuse, and insubordination at work, that is all we need to know. We might be (perhaps should be) interested at some point in the specifics of why a person responded in a particular way to an individual item on a personality measure (e.g., why a person would say "True" to the item "I prefer a shower to a tub bath"). However, the first question is, "Do the scores based on the measure predict anything useful?" This question got completely lost during the response set controversy and is still not asked as often as it should be.

Consider one more point about social desirability. The developmental process known as socialization concerns persuading children to stop doing as they please and begin acting in ways that please adults and the larger society. Part of what it means to be socialized is to behave in a socially desirable fashion, whether dining in public or responding to items on psychological questionnaires. All social behavior can be organized along a continuum of relative social desirability, and where an individual typically falls on this continuum is important information.

ACADEMIC CRITICISM OF PERSONALITY: *WELTANSCHAUNG* FACTOR NUMBER 1

In addition to its self-inflicted wounds, personality psychology suffered from the generally hostile intellectual and cultural climate (*weltanschaung*) of American psychology between 1960 and 1990. There are at least three distinct factors that contributed to the hostile climate. The first was the collateral damage caused by the publication of Jensen's (1969) vastly influential *Harvard Educational Review* article. Jensen argued that there are reliable Black–White differences on measures of cognitive ability; that Whites tend to score higher than Blacks; and finally, that these differences are genetic, innate, and built in. Jensen's paper created a firestorm of protest from liberal intellectuals and scientists everywhere, and he was subsequently subjected to the most intense kind of harassment from precisely the section of the population—academics—who are allegedly most in favor of free speech. Officials at the University of California at Berkeley, where Jensen worked, hired armed guards to protect him on campus.

Although a review of Jensen's work is not directly relevant to the goals of this chapter, it would be useful to note the following points. Jensen's arguments follow logically from his data, a point that his critics still dispute. However, in my view Jensen's data do not support the conclusion that there are innate Black–White differences in intelligence. There are three problems with his conclusion. First, Jensen defines intelligence in terms of scores on existing measures of cognitive ability; that is, he defines intelligence as that which intelligence tests test—which is obviously circular. The circularity of this definition undermines Jensen's evidence for innate Black–White differences in cognitive ability. Second, there is the so-called Flynn effect (Flynn, 1999). Flynn provided very powerful data showing that IQ scores (in every population that he studied) increase by about 1 *SD* every 30 years. This raises serious questions about whether conventional IQ tests measure a stable, enduring capacity that is under genetic control. Third, Gottlieb (2000) and others have argued that the heritability coefficient that psychologists use to estimate genetic influence on test scores is inappropriate. This heritability index was developed by geneticists to predict the outcome of breeding experiments (usually with mice). The index was never intended to be used (as psychologists do) to divide the total variance of an expressed trait (scores on IQ tests) into that caused by genes and that which is determined by environment.

What does this have to do with personality psychology? The Jensen argument became a problem for personality psychology because many prominent early personality psychologists (e.g., McDougall and Cattell) believed that there are distinct human races, that the differences between the races were genetic, and that innate differences between people could be measured with personality inventories. The situation was made worse by the widespread belief that personality inventories measure traits, a term that implies the existence of underlying genetic causes. Moreover, personality psychology has been closely linked with human behavior genetics and evolutionary theory over the past 30 years (Buss, 1997). Finally, personality psychologists have also used the standard heritability index to estimate the genetic loading of traits for almost 40 years (cf. Rowe, 1997). All of this suggested that personality psychology carried the same implicit racist claims that liberals had attributed to Jensen, and this drew down the wrath of liberals on personality psychology in general.

ACADEMIC CRITICISM OF PERSONALITY: *WELTANSCHAUNG* FACTOR NUMBER 2

The second cultural factor that negatively influenced personality psychology was the neo-Romantic movement that swept the United States beginning after World War II, and gained great momentum in the 1960s. Fueled by a belief in the possibilities of human progress and the capacity for individual self-enhancement, trainers and psychotherapists preached the gospel of continuous personal growth. Along with many academic psychologists, New Age therapists denied the existence of stable structures inside the psyche, and extolled the virtue of constant self-reinvention—a virtue that is embraced by every politician who gets in trouble. The most fundamental claim of personality psychology is that people's behavior reflects the influence of underlying and stable structures (however, these structures may be defined). This view of stable structures lends itself to conservative political arguments; for example, because, in principle, criminals cannot be reformed, the solution to crime is better prisons. Permanent growth and self-development are only possible if the psychological structures inside people are fluid and malleable. Hence, the popular New Age psychology of the 1960s and 1970s was fundamentally hostile to traditional conceptions of personality.

ACADEMIC CRITICISM OF PERSONALITY: *WELTANSCHAUNG* FACTOR NUMBER 3

The third source of academic criticism was, and is, behaviorism. There is an important pragmatic emphasis to behaviorism—the useful part of the behaviorist argument is that we should not care what people say, or claim that they feel; we should care about what they actually do. I absolutely agree with this principle. However, the behaviorists go further and argue that (a) what people do depends on the situations they are in; (b) the fact that people's actions reflect the situations they are in means that there are no stable structures inside people that determine or explain their actions (i.e., there is no such thing as personality); and (c) because there are no stable structures inside people, personality assessment is meaningless. Behaviorism is fundamentally critical of personality psychology, and behaviorism is often the unexamined basis for much thinking in social and industrial psychology.

The fundamental intellectual claim of behaviorism and traditional social psychology is that individual action is primarily determined by social circumstances. The first major study in the history of social psychology involved demonstrating that a bicyclist performed better when observed by an audience—from the rear of a moving train (cf. Allport, 1954). The seldom-read but often-cited Hawthorne studies (Roethlisberger & Dickson, 1939) provided a highly visible example of the power of situations in a real work environment. Subsequent research in social psychology often consists of different demonstrations of how people's actions are influenced by situational factors.

In the 1960s, the social psychologists mounted a relentless attack on personality psychology. It would take us too far afield to document the full extent of this attack. I mention two highlights here. The first was a series of experiments that seemed to show the haplessness of individuals in the face of social pressure, indicating that personality was only a trivial causal factor in human affairs. The most famous of these demonstrations is the Milgram (1963) conformity experiment. In this dramatic study, Milgram showed that 80% of volunteers recruited off the street in New Haven, Connecticut, were willing to administer lethal doses of an electrical shock to a stranger in the context of what seemed to be a medical experiment. This seemed to be an extraordinary example of how personality was a trivial factor influencing everyday social behavior.

The second highlight was Mischel's (1968) book, which crystallized antipersonality sentiment and became the bible of the personality critics. The key argument of Mischel's book and the situationist critique of personality can be summarized quite succinctly. Mischel argued that if personality exists, behavior should be consistent across situations. He then reviewed the research literature prior to 1968 and concluded that it contained very little evidence to support the notion that individual behavior is consistent across situations. He concluded, therefore, that situational influences, and not personality, control individual behavior. Mischel then reviewed the results of certain well-known, large-scale assessment studies of the 1950s and 1960s and concluded that correlations between personality measures and real-world performance rarely exceed .30. He famously decreed that this correlation was the upper limit for the validity of personality assessment.

Mischel's book launched the so-called person–situation debate (Kenrick & Funder, 1988) that further paralyzed personality research for about 15 years. In retrospect, the tremendous impact of the book seems odd, given the premises on which it is based. Consider Mischel's claim: If personality exists, then behavior should be consistent across situations. First, why is consistent behavior the test for the existence of personality? Why not use consistent intentions, consistent values, or consistent goals? Giving someone the finger and sticking one's tongue out at the person are different behaviors, but both acts signify consistent intentions. Second, what does consistent mean? The problem of defining consistency is one of the oldest and most intractable in philosophy. By requiring personality psychology to demonstrate an indeterminate degree of consistency in behavior, Mischel sent the discipline on a fool's errand, searching for something that cannot be found in principle. Third, as of today, social psychologists have yet to provide a coherent definition of a situation (cf. Hogan & Roberts, 2000), which means that, by Mischel's test, behavior is required to be consistent across a set of conditions that are undefined.

THE REBIRTH OF PERSONALITY

All of these factors—the social desirability response set controversy, the suspicion that personality psychology is racist, the New Age belief in the need and possibility for continuous personal renewal, and the animus of behavioristic social psychology—served to drive personality psychology out of the realm of scientific and intellectual respectability by the mid-1970s. However, since the early 1990s, personality psychology has experienced a dramatic comeback (cf. Roberts & Hogan, 2001). The reasons for the comeback have nothing to do with new-found agreement within academic psychology. There is an old academic joke to the effect that, if you stacked all of the economists in the world end to end, they still would not reach a conclusion. The same is true for psychologists, whose great debates are never resolved; they are merely ignored after a time. Like the 100 Years War, at some point, people simply became tired of fighting.

The rebirth of personality psychology was largely stimulated by demands from the business community, although academic research played a part at the beginning. We can trace five lines of influence that led to the current enthusiasm for personality assessment and research. The first was a consequence of the development of the FFM (Wiggins, 1996). The FFM argues that individual differences in social behavior, and the structure of personality measurement data, can be adequately described in terms of five broad dimensions (called Adjustment, Ascendance, Agreeableness, Prudence, and Intellect/Openness). Adjustment is the topic that interested Freud and Jung because the low end of Adjustment concerns neuroticism. Ascendance is defined in terms of active engagement in the world, and the search for stimulation and social interaction. Agreeableness involves warmth, charm, tact, and social skill. Prudence is expressed in terms of rule following, dependability, and obedience to authority. Intellect/Openness concerns creativity and imagination. The FFM provides an agreed-on taxonomy of the major dimensions of personality. Moreover, an overwhelming body of research shows that the many (thousands of) different measures of personality that exist today all assess these same five dimensions with varying degrees of adequacy and efficiency. In addition, the FFM has been replicated in languages and cultures all over the world (McCrae & Costa, 1997). There is abundant evidence to suggest that scores on measures of the FFM are heritable and stable over time (Costa & McCrae, 1988). Finally, the FFM provides a common vocabulary for talking about personality. With the FFM, a new sheriff came to town, instilling a measure of order in a notoriously lawless group discussion.

The second factor that paved the way for the rebirth of personality psychology was a major piece of legislation—the Civil Rights Act of 1964. Title VII of this act forbids discrimination in employment. In 1972, the Equal Employment Opportunity Commission (EEOC) was given power of enforcement of the Civil Rights Act. In a dramatic gesture that caught the attention of employers and human resource managers nationwide, the EEOC successfully sued AT&T in 1973 for discriminatory hiring practices. Many employers used physical ability tests to screen women out of jobs traditionally held by men, and they used cognitive ability measures to screen out Blacks from jobs traditionally held by Whites. The EEOC guidelines for employee selection triggered a search for alternative selection procedures with equal validity but less adverse impact. This search led inexorably to personality measurement because well-constructed personality measures have no adverse impact on women or minorities, and older people tend to score better than younger people.

The requirement to find alternative selection procedures with less adverse impact than measures of cognitive ability, combined with the newly discovered FFM, led I/O psychologists to begin reevaluating the validity of personality measures for personnel selection, and this reevaluation was the third factor that led to the rebirth of personality psychology. In the early 1990s, consensus began rapidly building around the notion that well-constructed measures of personality predicted occupational performance about as well as measures of cognitive ability. For example, in a study of personality and occupational performance, Hogan and Holland (2003), using meta-analytic procedures and very large samples, reported the following estimated true validities for the dimensions of the FFM: Adjustment = .43, Ascendance = .35, Agreeableness = .34, Prudence = .36, and Intellect/Openness = .34. Similarly, in a study of the links between personality and leadership, Judge, Bono, Ilies, and Gerhardt (2002) reported the following estimated true validities for the dimensions of the FFM: Adjustment = −.24, Ascendance = .31, Agreeableness = .08, Prudence = .28, and Intellect/Openness = .24. They also reported a multiple correlation between the FFM and leadership of .48.

Findings such as these have created a huge groundswell of enthusiasm for the use of personality measures in preemployment screening. Such findings have also generated great enthusiasm for personality research in applied psychology. However, once again, the demand for the research and the enthusiasm for the results came from the business community, not from academic psychology. Smart psychological consultants quickly realized they had a new product to sell to their clients—personality-based personnel selection—and they began to do so.

The fourth factor that has contributed to the reemergence of personality psychology concerns the business world's discovery of the Myers–Briggs Type Indicator (MBTI; Myers & McCauley, 1985) and the notion of emotional intelligence (EQ; Goleman, 1995). The MBTI contains four scales: Introversion– Extraversion, Sensation–Intuition, Thinking–Feeling, and Judging–Perceiving. The measure is based on Jung's ideas about how cognitive information processing influences personality. The four scales are used to sort people into 16 types; the types themselves are characterized by certain values, preferences, and cognitive styles. Information about a person's type is then used for career guidance, team building, and other activities associated with organizational development. Most personality psychologists regard the MBTI as little more than an elaborate Chinese fortune cookie—each of the 16 MBTI types is described in a chirpy and upbeat fashion as having important and distinctive qualities. Nonetheless, psychological consultants have discovered that the business community has an endless appetite for MBTI-based feedback. Since 1975, the MBTI has become one of the best-selling psychological tests of all time. Although academics are baffled and annoyed by the astonishing popularity of the MBTI, MBTI feedback is harmless and it provides a nice income for many consultants. However, the important thing about the MBTI that many personality psychologists overlook is that its sheer popularity has served to legitimize the concept of personality assessment in the business community.

What the MBTI is to team building, EQ is to leadership. Goleman (1995) defined EQ as the ability to manage oneself and one's relations effectively, and said it has four components: self-awareness, self-management, social awareness, and social skill. EQ is thought to be important for leadership because persons who lack it alienate their staff and coworkers and ultimately thwart their own careers. Kouzes and Posner (2002), in their highly successful treatise on leadership, described EQ as "no passing fad" (p. 284) and as "serious stuff" (p. 285). As they noted:

> Senior executives can graduate at the top of the best business schools, reason circles around their brightest peers, solve technical problems with wizard-like powers, have the relevant situational, functional, and in-

dustry experience, and still be more likely to fail than succeed—unless they also possess the requisite personal and social skills. (p. 285)

The EQ movement has taken the world of leadership training by storm; it has become vastly popular and quite profitable. Academic psychologists regard this development with dismay, noting that Goleman's concept is internally inconsistent, and that the various methods available for measuring it will not pass technical scrutiny (Hogan & Stokes, 2006). Nonetheless, the EQ concept speaks to two important home truths that have largely eluded many academics. The first is that many people in the business community have always believed that personality influences occupational performance, even though academic psychology has disputed this belief. The second home truth is that many people in the business community have always understood that there is more to leadership performance than IQ, even though academic psychology disputed this notion as well.

The final factor that contributed to the rebirth of personality psychology is the competency movement, which I describe in detail in chapter 7. For the moment, let me simply note that the competency movement developed as a reaction to traditional, behaviorist job analysis methods applied to the study of managerial performance, and the competency movement was originally inspired by McClelland, a personality psychologist.

As a final observation, it is ironic to note that the degree to which a person recognizes the importance of personality at work is itself a personality test. There is a kind of person who reliably discounts the relevance of personality when thinking about performance. These people typically come from accounting, finance, or engineering; they are people with strong backgrounds and interests in technical matters. Similarly, within academic psychology, the critics largely come from the technical subdisciplines. They tend to be smart, tough-minded, critical, and introverted, all of which makes them effective critics.

This chapter has traced the fall and reemergence of personality psychology in modern intellectual life. I noted that personality psychology virtually disappeared in the late 1970s, due to a convergence of forces within and without academia. I then noted that there has been a remarkable resurgence of interest in personality psychology since 1990. This resurgence is a result of developments in business and applied psychology, rather than academic psychology. The resurgence has been largely stimulated by consultants who realized they could sell assessment results to the business community. To summarize this chapter, the reason personality psychology went away had more to do with academic politics than it did with data and logic. Similarly, the return of personality psychology has had more to do with the economics of consulting than with data and logic. Although data and logic have always supported the utility of personality psychology, it did not matter. Nils Bohr, who won a Nobel Prize for Physics in 1922, once noted that, in science you never persuade your critics, you just wait for them to die.

3

Who Shall Rule?
Leadership and Personality

All primates, including humans, live in groups, and the groups are organized in terms of dominance hierarchies. However, humans have evolved beyond the simple hierarchical groups that characterize, for example, the chimpanzees, our closest primate relative. Humans have developed formal social organizations that allow them to accomplish sophisticated goals that are not attainable by individuals or mobs. The first significant social organizations were hunting bands and war parties; these groups, which initially must have resembled those formed by chimpanzees, were key elements in human survival. People evolved as group-living animals, and that has important consequences for understanding social behavior in general and leadership in particular—because people are prewired for group living.

Humans developed agriculture after the end of the last ice age (11,000 years ago; cf. Diamond, 1997); this was a transforming event because people then moved into the first settled communities, and acquired organized religion and social organizations dominated by priests and warlords, often working together. In the Western world, these living arrangements continued until the 19th century when, with the advent of the Industrial Revolution, they began to break down, at least in the industrialized West. The Industrial Revolution led to the modern business organization and the subsequent evolution of large business systems. Nonetheless, modern organizations share many features of the earlier social organizations, including hierarchical structures, division of labor, reporting relationships, coalition building, betrayals, and constant maneuvering for power. Moreover, social groups dominated by warlords seem to be the default position for human societies—witness how quickly they emerged in Iraq after the fall of Saddam Hussein and how common they are in underdeveloped countries such as Afghanistan and Ethiopia.

People occupy different positions in the hierarchies in which they live and work, and the positions have varying levels of power and authority. The term *manager* refers to position holders in modern organizations. The duties of managers differ depending on their level in an organization, and with the major activities and goals of their organizations. Nonetheless, all managerial jobs have one important feature in common: They help accomplish the work of an organization through other people. This means that managers are responsible for the performance of their staffs.

DEFINING LEADERSHIP

It is fashionable to distinguish managers from leaders: Managers are supposed to do things right, whereas leaders are supposed to do the right thing. However, this distinction is too facile. The word *leadership* has two meanings. On the one hand, leadership refers to a certain kind of position in an organization—a leadership position. On the other hand, leadership refers to a kind of performance—behaving in a leader-like way. The existence of these two definitions means that they are independent; there are people in leadership positions who do not behave as leaders, and there are people who are not in leadership positions who nonetheless exercise leadership. By definition, managers are in positions of leadership; whether they exercise it appropriately is another question.

Leadership is the most important topic in the social, behavioral, and organizational sciences. When good leadership prevails, organizations and people prosper. Bad leadership is almost always accompanied by disasters. Consider the career of Foday Sankoh, the former dictator of Sierra Leone, who died in July 2003. Sankoh was born in 1937 and grew up in a Sierra Leone that was dominated by a small, corrupt urban elite he deeply resented. He joined the Sierra Leonean army, took part in a failed coup attempt in 1971, and was sent to prison for 7 years. In 1978 he went to Libya to train with other West African revolutionaries; there he met Charles Taylor (the recently deposed dictator of Liberia) who became Sankoh's major ally. On returning to Sierra Leone, Sankoh founded the Revolutionary United Front (RUF) with the intention of overthrowing the Sierra Leonean government and taking over the country's diamond mines.

Sankoh was bright, charming, and charismatic, and he quickly attracted a large popular following, primarily among the teenaged underclass. He promised to reform education, health care, and other public services, and to distribute the revenues from the sale of diamonds. Instead, he used the revenues to turn the RUF into an army, to buy arms (from Charles Taylor), and to buy other political support. He paid his army irregularly because he expected his soldiers to live by looting and even by cannibalizing their victims. New recruits were sometimes required to murder their own parents, which toughened them and made it hard for them to return home. His young soldiers, deprived of parenting and raised in murderous chaos, were notoriously savage, and specialized in amputating appendages, which they kept in bags. Those with the most body parts were rewarded. By the end of the 1990s, Sierra Leone was, according to the United Nations, the poorest country on earth. To stop the slaughter and ameliorate the misery, the United Nations, after several false starts, intervened in 2000. Sankoh was taken captive by an emboldened mob, after they were fired on by his bodyguards. He was subsequently indicted by an international court for crimes against humanity. While in prison he lost his mind, then had a stroke and died of a pulmonary embolism, leaving his impoverished country and its mutilated citizenry finally in peace.

Sadly, the moral of this story—that bad leaders cause much misery—is all too common. If you put on a blindfold, throw a dart at a map of the world, and then move to whatever country the dart lands on, there is about a 70% probability that you would be moving to a dictatorship. Leadership is the most important problem in the social sciences.

Historically, leadership has been conceptualized in two very different ways. On the one hand, in a tradition extending from Hegel through Marx and Durkheim to modern sociologists and social psychologists, some people argue that leaders are created by their roles and by historical, economic, and institutional circumstances. The most noteworthy advocates of this view are governments and military organizations;

these agencies believe that when a person is placed in a leadership role, that person is, by definition, a leader, and that these people are fungible—It does not particularly matter who is in the role because individual differences in the talent for leadership are irrelevant.

On the other hand, in a tradition extending from Freud and Weber to me, people argue that leadership is a function of the characteristics of individuals. This means that some people have more talent for leadership than others and that view is the premise of this book. The assumption that leadership is related to personality seems commonsensical; nonetheless, it has been the topic of furious academic debate over the years.

How should leadership be defined? Psychologists and business book authors typically define leadership in terms of whoever is in charge. The senior officials in the U.S. government are leaders, as are the senior executives at General Motors and Microsoft. But think for a moment about what is required to negotiate successfully the status hierarchy of a large, male-dominated, bureaucratic organization. Think about the people who are in charge of the organization where you work, and try to recall examples of real leadership. The people who rise to the tops of large organizations are distinguished by hard work, brains, ambition, political skill, and luck, but not necessarily by a talent for leadership.

As an alternative way to conceptualize leadership, think for a moment about human origins (cf. Boehm, 1999). As noted, people evolved as group-living animals—because there is safety in numbers. Over the 2 million years of human prehistory, the various hominid groups were in competition, each group sought constantly to appropriate the resources of the others, and the competition was quite savage. If a particular group was overrun, the losers were killed, eaten, or otherwise dispersed, and they then disappeared from the gene pool. For example, when Genghis Khan invaded Persia, he killed every human inhabitant (DeHartog, 2000). Despite the external threats, people are naturally selfish; left to their own devices, they will pursue their short-term self-interests. In the context of the violent tribal warfare that has characterized most of human history, survival and fitness depended on both individual capabilities and the defensive capabilities of one's group; thus, leadership was (and is) a resource for group survival—leadership is a collective phenomena (Avolio, Sosik, Jung, & Berson, 2003). This holds a key to the definition of leadership.

Leadership should be defined in terms of the ability to build and maintain a group that performs well compared to its competition. Leadership should be evaluated in terms of the performance of the group over time (Hogan, Curphy, & Hogan, 1994). This definition departs from the conventional wisdom of leadership studies, most of which define leadership in terms of emergence—the person in a group of strangers who exerts the most influence—or in terms of ratings of an individual leader by more senior leaders. Although very few studies have used indexes of group performance as a criterion, it is the most appropriate way to define and evaluate leadership.

LEADERSHIP CHARACTERISTICS

If we say that leadership is a function of individual characteristics (i.e., personality), the next question is what those characteristics are. Here matters get seriously murky. The published literature on leadership is immense—actually overwhelming—and growing daily. This literature falls neatly into two camps that I call the troubadour tradition and the academic tradition. The *troubadour tradition* is by far the largest. It consists of such amiable works of pop fiction as *Leadership Lessons of Genghis Khan, Leadership Lessons of Jesus Christ,* and *Leadership Lessons of Abraham Lincoln.* It also consists of the opinions and score-settling reminiscences of self-promoting former chief executive officers (CEOs). These works have high entertainment value, but they contain few defensible empirical generalizations.

In contrast with the troubadour tradition, the *academic tradition* contains many solid empirical nuggets such as "Leaders tend to be slightly taller than their subordinates." Generally speaking, however, the academic tradition is a collection of decontextualized facts that do not add up to a persuasive account of leadership. In addition, the academic study of leadership is as often swept by fads as the popular music industry. From the perspective of a nonacademic person trying to understand leadership, there are two problems with the academic tradition: Many of the insights are relatively trivial and only a few of the insights replicate—there is little agreement across empirical studies regarding the defining characteristics of leadership.

What We Know About Leadership

What do we know, in a reliable way, about leadership when it is defined in terms of the ability to build and maintain a successful team? A careful reading of the literature suggests that we know at least six things.

1. *A leader is a leader is a leader.* The published literature on leadership extends to well over 8,000 books and articles. People who write about leadership emphasize the distinctiveness of their viewpoints. In reality there is remarkable sameness across the literature in both the troubadour and academic traditions in the way they characterize the attributes of effective leaders. Effective leaders tend to be resilient and handle stress well, they promote a vision and develop strategies to translate the vision into reality, they solve tactical and strategic problems, they set high goals and work hard to achieve them, they project a sense of self-confidence, they build relationships, they build teams, they follow through on their commitments and treat people fairly, and they plan and organize work. These attributes are no guarantee of success, but they improve the odds of a person being able to build a high-performing team that achieves results.

What is even more interesting is that the characteristics associated with effective leadership are surprisingly similar across industries and cultures. Organizations (and countries) like to argue that they are perfectly unique, and indeed they will pay consultants to tell them how unique they are. In reality, however, the basic building blocks of leadership are the same across organizations. In the best study yet published on the personality determinants of leadership, Judge, Bono, Ilies, and Gerhardt (2002) examined 78 studies of the relation between personality and leadership, using meta-analysis. They defined and organized personality in each study in terms of the FFM. They then classified the leadership criteria in the 78 studies in terms of emergence and effectiveness. They reported that all five dimensions of personality predicted overall leadership (emergence and effectiveness combined) with true correlations of .24 or greater for every dimension except agreeableness (.08). The multiple R for all five dimensions predicting emergence was .53, and .39 for predicting their criteria of effectiveness (see Hogan & Hogan, 2002a; Lord, DeVader, & Alliger, 1986, for similar results). What constitutes good leadership in a Chinese manufacturing facility will closely resemble good leadership in a French agricultural cooperative or a U.S. Internet company.

2. *Executive failure.* The second thing we know is that perhaps two thirds of the people currently in leadership positions in corporate America will fail; they will then be fired, demoted, or kicked upstairs. The most common reason for their failure will be their inability to build or maintain a team. Their inability to build a team is

typically a function of certain dysfunctional interpersonal tendencies that are hard to detect during job interviews or assessment center exercises. Interpersonal tendencies are, of course, a direct reflection of personality. The topic of managerial derailment is discussed in detail in chapter 6.

Consider the case of Philip J. Purcell, who was fired as CEO of Morgan Stanley, an investment banking firm, in June 2005. Purcell was originally employed by McKinsey, an East Coast consulting firm. He did some early work with Dean Witter (a stock brokerage firm in Chicago), then became CEO in the late 1970s. In 1997, he orchestrated a merger with Morgan Stanley (in New York), a merger that was widely questioned at the time on the grounds of poor culture fit. Although he initially agreed to share power with the former CEO of Morgan Stanley, he quickly forced him out of the organization. In 2005, the *New York Times* described Mr. Purcell as ruthless, autocratic, and remote, with no tolerance for dissent or even argument. He pushed away strong people and surrounded himself with "yes" men and women. He demanded loyalty to himself over the organization. He played power games, lived in Chicago, had little contact with the Morgan Stanley rank and file in New York, stayed in his office and plotted "strategy." "He belittled the investment bankers [at Morgan Stanley]. Executives learned that it was pointless to argue with Mr. Purcell about anything—all it did was make him mad and he didn't even pretend to be listening." Disgusted top executives from Morgan Stanley began leaving in droves, and Purcell used their departures as a chance to give their jobs to people who were loyal to him. Former Morgan Stanley executives, infuriated by the way they had been treated, created enough shareholder agitation, and made it clear that they would not quit, so the Morgan Stanley board fired Purcell the week of June 13, but only after the stock had suffered tremendous losses and the company had lost some of the most talented investment bankers in the industry.

Why, you might ask, do so many executives fail? Obviously there will be several reasons—circumstances, luck, war, natural disasters, and other factors beyond individual control. However, one reason for their failure that is under our control concerns how they are selected and hired (Sessa, Kaiser, Taylor, & Campbell, 1998). Formal selection tools are rarely used. Former subordinates—people who are best able to comment on a person's talent for leadership—are almost never consulted. New executives are often recruited from outside the organization, making it even harder to evaluate them because there is no track record or institutional memory. The most common selection tool is an interview; narcissists and psychopaths excel during interviews. Thus I believe many executives are hired based on characteristics that are irrelevant to their success as leaders.

3. *Employee dissatisfaction.* The third thing that we know is that bad management is the primary cause of employee dissatisfaction—the best predictor of employee dissatisfaction is poor leadership. It is important to remember that measures of employee dissatisfaction are substantially correlated with a wide range of undesirable business outcomes (e.g., theft, absenteeism, turnover, etc.; cf. Harter, Schmidt, & Hayes, 2002). In a sample of 1,030 hourly employees in a large East Coast grocery firm, I conducted a set of analyses to identify the sources of turnover. In this sample, the base rate of turnover in a 60-day interval was 23%; 3% of the turnover was involuntary and 20% was voluntary.

The sample could be divided into four broad job types—cashiers, stockers, clerks, and managers—and turnover differed across these jobs. The turnover rate for managers was 4% (far below the base rate), whereas the turnover rate for stockers was 32% (far above the base rate). The most interesting results came from the cashier job. Turnover rates for cashiers at different locations varied by more than 35 percentage points; this suggested that the quality of supervision was driving turnover. I identified four supervisors who were classified as high fit based on their personality scores. The turnover rate for cashiers working for these supervisors was 6%, as compared with a turnover rate of 21% for all cashiers. In addition, one group of cashiers had a turnover rate of 36%. A new manager was hired, and the turnover rate fell to 4%. This is good evidence that bad managers create turnover—people do not quit organizations, they quit bad bosses.

4. *Implicit models of leadership.* At various points in this volume I have argued that discussions of personality should distinguish between identity (a person's self-view) and reputation (how the person is seen by others). The fourth thing we know about leadership concerns leader reputation: There are certain things that people want to see in leaders and persons lacking these characteristics will have trouble establishing their credibility to be in charge. In order of importance, four themes regularly come up: integrity, decisiveness, competence, and vision (cf. Kouzes & Posner, 2002; Lord, Foti, & DeVader, 1984).

The first and most important theme concerns credibility as a leader, and this vitally depends on perceived integrity—keeping one's word, fulfilling one's promises, not playing favorites, not taking advantage of one's position, and not claiming special privileges. The first question asked of potential leaders is can they be trusted not to abuse the privilege of authority. A meta-analysis by Dirks and Ferrin (2002) shows reliable correlations between trust in a supervisor and a range of positive outcomes, including improved job performance, job satisfaction, and organizational commitment.

The second theme concerns decisiveness. Good leaders make sound, defensible decisions in a timely way, especially in times of crisis and uncertainty (Vroom & Jago, 1988; Yukl, 1998). Naval historians point to the quality of Horatio Nelson's decision making under the incredibly difficult and confusing conditions of a sea battle as an index of his greatness (Pocock, 1987). However, decisiveness is just as important in more mundane circumstances. Mintzberg (1973) noted that managers are involved in constant decision making; the quality of their decisions accumulates and determines the fate of the organization.

The next theme concerns competence. Good leaders seem competent; they are obviously good at some aspects of the business—they are resources for the team in achieving its goals. In hunter-gatherer societies—which are ferociously democratic—the head man is usually distinguished by superior hunting skills and a broader moral perspective (cf. Boehm, 1999). Expertise is needed for legitimacy and respect from the team (French & Raven, 1959); the fact that colleges and universities are typically led by failed academics partially explains their problems with faculty morale.

Finally, good leaders are perceived as visionary—they can explain why the team's activity is important and how it contributes to the future success and well-being of the members. Napoleon noted that "leaders are dealers in hope," and vision is their currency. George H. W. Bush, the 41st president of the United States, lost the 1992 election to Bill Clinton in part because Bush, a bright but very pragmatic man, could offer no convincing reason why he should be reelected and complained to his staff that he did not understand "this vision thing."

5. *Good to great themes.* Most business books are empirical nonsense, but Collins's (2001) book, *Good to Great,* is an exception. He and his staff searched databases for the *Fortune* 1000 companies to identify firms that had 15 years of performance below the average of

their business sector, then 15 years of sustained performance significantly above the average of their sector. They found 11 companies
that fit this profile. The next question became what distinguished
these 11 companies. The somewhat reluctant conclusion was that the
distinguishing feature was a new CEO who took charge of the organization and then dramatically improved its performance.

Beyond the four themes (integrity, decisiveness, competence, and
vision) already described, these 11 CEOs shared the same two additional characteristics. First, they were modest and humble, as opposed
to self-dramatizing and charismatic. Second, they were phenomenally,
almost preternaturally, persistent. These findings were a jolt to the
business literature (which promotes the cult of the charismatic CEO),
but I think they make perfect sense when compared with the data provided by ethnographic studies of leadership (Boehm, 1999). In
hunter-gatherer societies, the head man is invariably modest, self-effac-
ing, competent, and committed to the collective good. If he is not, the
other members will remove him—sometimes quite violently.

6. *Changing demands of leadership.* Equitable Life, the world's
oldest life insurer located in the United Kingdom, nearly collapsed
in 2000. Vast sums of money were lost and major lawsuits followed.
The British government asked Lord Penrose, a Scottish judge, to determine the reasons for the sudden and unexpected failure of the
former star of the insurance industry. After more than 30 months of
investigation, Penrose published his report on March 8, 2004. Most
people thought the collapse was caused by an ill-advised government intervention. However, Penrose concluded that the government intervention was only the final straw, which came after years of
mismanagement, the most important cause of which was "actuarial
practices of dubious merit." The company's board had neither the
information nor the skill to deal with the firm's finances; Penrose
described the board as "startlingly incompetent." The board, in
turn, depended on "the actuary" for its information. The actuary
was Roy Ransom, who was also the CEO of Equitable Life. Penrose
described Ransom as "manipulative, obstructive, and dismissive."
Ransom left the firm and was not prosecuted. Leaders are leaders
are leaders, even when they are bad.

Despite the abundance of stories such as the foregoing, Kellerman
(2004) noted that to write a best-selling business book, one must compose a hymn in praise of the corporate elite—one needs to describe
the wondrous characteristics that set CEOs and other top managers

apart from the less talented people who serve them. Academic psychology also depicts senior managers in business as a race of heroes. I believe, however, that senior executives differ from junior managers in terms of (a) experience and political skill, (b) to whom they report, and (c) little else that is measurable. In a rare television interview in March 2004, William Rehnquist, Chief Justice of the U.S. Supreme Court, said the key to becoming Chief Justice is "to be there when the bus pulls up." This is probably what it takes to become a CEO.

A consistent theme in the professional literature is that, compared to lower level managers, senior managers are brighter, have a more differentiated behavioral repertoire, are more cognitively complex, and think in terms of longer time horizons (Antonakis & Atwater, 2002; Hunt, 1991; Zaccaro, 2001). All of these writers tell us that the skills and abilities of top-level leaders are qualitatively different from those at lower levels—executive leadership is leadership of organizations, whereas lower level leadership is leadership in organizations. However, I do not know of any data that support these claims. Obviously older managers are older and have had more experience than younger managers—that much seems obvious. More than that, however, remains to be demonstrated.

In the process of a large-scale succession management study with a multinational corporation, we gathered data from four levels of senior managers, all of whom were being evaluated for their potential to ultimately run the company ($N = 170$). There were four data sources: (a) data from our personality-based job analysis instrument; (b) scores on the Watson–Gleser Critical Thinking measure; (c) scores on the HPI, a measure of normal personality; and (d) scores on the Hogan Development Survey (HDS), a measure of derailment tendencies. The data analyses consisted of calculating and comparing mean scores on the various psychometric devices.

Data from the personality-based job analysis showed that, across the four levels, the managers described their jobs as requiring the same, and same level of, capabilities and competencies. Data from the Watson–Glaser clearly indicated no differences in psychometric intelligence across the four levels of management. The HPI was developed on working adults and designed to predict occupational performance. More than 1 million adults have completed the inventory, it has been used in more than 500 studies, it is an exceptionally well-validated measure of individual differences in occupational performance, and there were no differences in HPI scores across the four levels of management. Finally, the HDS is designed to forecast managerial derailment, which means that lower scores are better. There were no differences in mean scores across the scales of the HDS for the four groups of managers.

This is probably the largest single data set available to evaluate the notion that senior managers are more talented than junior managers. The data plainly support the conclusion that there are virtually no differences in managers across four levels in this very large corporation in terms of required competencies, measured cognitive ability, normal personality, or dysfunctional personality characteristics. The data also indicate that good managers differed from poor managers in consistent and measurable ways, independent of the managerial level; good managers were the same at each level.

Psychologists who consult with business are under considerable financial pressure to tell their clients interesting stories about their corporate capabilities, but it is equally important to tell them a true story. I believe that this group has a moral obligation to speak truth to power.

THE TIES THAT BIND

The links or ties that bind leaders and followers is a topic that deserves more scrutiny than it has received. There are three models for understanding these links. The first comes from Freud, the founder of psychoanalysis, and Weber, the great German sociologist. Both argued that leaders exert a kind of spell over their followers. Leaders and followers are linked by emotional bonds, created in part by the compelling (charismatic) personalities of the leaders, and in part by the primitive emotional needs of the followers. Inspired by Weber, modern discussions of transformational leadership are in the direct line of descent of this tradition, which holds that followers are linked to leaders through a combination of the personal characteristics of the leaders and the private needs of the followers. It is interesting to note that, after all these years, there are Germans who long for Hitler's return, Italians who long for Mussolini, Argentines who long for Juan Peron, Russians who long for Stalin, and Chinese who long for Mao.

I have suggested a second model, based on the view that the primary task of leaders is to build a group, persuade the individuals to work together, and then maintain their performance. Leaders recruit and bind people to a team in two ways. First, they are able to build stable relationships with individual members—this is largely a function of their integrity and social skill. Conversely, poor leaders, who often lack social skill or integrity, are unable to build relationships, and therefore to build and maintain effective work groups. The second way leaders are able to bind people to a team is by providing participants with a credible rationale for their membership. Effective leaders are able to project a vision that the individuals find attractive, a vision that is consistent with their own identities and gives some meaning and purpose to their participation in the team task. In summary, in this view, people are linked to groups by virtue of the personality of the leader: Leaders with social skill and integrity are able to recruit individuals, in a psychological sense, to group participation. Those who lack social skill or integrity can only form a group by demanding the obedience of their staff, and such groups are generally ineffective. Leaders with imagination can project a vision that participants find attractive, morally compelling, and worthy of allegiance, whereas incompetent leaders unwittingly project visions that are distasteful (incongruent with identity or status motivations) to people.

A third model for interpreting the links between leaders and subordinates comes from evolutionary theory. Some theorists argue that leadership is a by-product of dominance and submission (Nicholson, 2000; Wilson, 1975). In groups, individuals compete for resources and this results in a hierarchy in which the dominant individual has greater access to resources than the subordinate members. Dominants can more or less do what they like in the group, and sometimes they do things that resemble leadership.

There are several problems with this by-product theory. First, dominant people do not need subordinates to achieve their goals; however, in pursuing their goals, they sometimes create opportunities for others. Dominant behavior is inconsistent with the view that leadership involves influencing others to achieve mutual goals. Furthermore, in human groups, there are severe limits to what dominants can achieve. In hunter-gatherer groups, members typically keep dominants under control, and if they persist in their bullying, the group punishes them (Boehm, 1999). Finally, leadership and dominance are weakly related (cf. Hogan & Hogan, 2001), so that measures of leadership and dominance correlate only modestly (Bass, 1990). In laboratory tasks, groups seldom choose a dominant group member as their leader (Van Vugt & De Cremer, 1999).

An alternative theory is that leadership evolved for the purpose of solving problems of group coordination. The need for concerted, collective action requires that someone initiate action and others follow. Individual differences in energy, knowledge, and ability make some individuals more likely to emerge as leaders. Leadership then evolved by virtue of its benefits for both leaders and followers in improving group coordination. This account of leadership can be illustrated by evolutionary game theory.

Evolutionary game theory (Maynard-Smith, 1982) can be used to model the evolution of social behaviors. It treats social interactions as "games" in which rational agents make decisions on the basis of the costs and benefits of available options. The agents embody strategies that, over the course of evolution, are tested against alternative strategies in terms of their relative (reproductive) success. Strategies (genes) spread through a population by virtue of the superior decision rules they adopt, whereas inferior strategies go extinct. This resembles natural selection (Dawkins, 1976).

The game of leader can serve as a model for the evolution of leadership (Rapoport, 1967). The simplest version involves two players, 1 and 2, each with two strategies, lead or follow. This yields four cells each with two payoffs (i.e., reproductive benefits or costs). The first payoff is always for Player 1 and the second for Player 2. If both choose to follow, they receive a zero payoff, and if both choose to lead, they receive a negative payoff. Players can solve the problem only if they coordinate their actions so that one player leads and the other follows. The leader then gets a larger payoff and the follower gets a smaller one, but they both profit. Leading is also the riskier option, because if both choose it, they both receive negative payoffs.

The leader–follower combinations are referred to as the game equilibria. Once interactions settle into either one of these combinations, they stay there. There might be occasional deviations from the equilibrium (e.g., when two leaders meet) but the payoffs ensure that a mixed leader–follower strategy evolves. The logic of the game is such that a leader–follower combination always does better than any combination of two leaders or followers. This implies that leader and follower roles might have coevolved across time, resulting in a stable distribution of leader and follower "genes" across a population (Maynard-Smith, 1982; Wilson et al., 1996).

Leadership theories typically assume that leaders and followers pursue shared goals (Fiedler, 1967; Hogg, 2001). In reality, however, there are frequent conflicts between them. In evolutionary theory, the criteria for success concern how well individuals do relative to others (Barrett et al., 2002). In nature, competition is likely to be the rule and cooperation the exception. Humans are unusual in that the benefits of cooperation are so substantial that we have evolved into an ultrasocial species (Van Vugt & Van Lange, in press). Nevertheless, human nature is at best ambivalent, and social behavior inevitably varies between cooperation and competition (Boehm, 1999; Hogan, 1982).

There are at least two reasons why leader–follower relations are ambivalent. First, not everyone with leadership aspirations becomes a leader. In any reasonably large population, several individuals will be competing for leadership positions (Nicholson, 2000). Through a complex process in which luck and circumstances play a major role, one individual will prevail over his or her competitors. Unless these competitors are physically removed from the group, they will lick their wounds and plan future opportunities to seize power. Second, coordinated group actions often lead to unequal outcomes such that leaders benefit more than followers. Leaders typically want to retain or increase their relative benefits, whereas followers want to reduce their relative losses. This tension creates selection pressures for self-serving behaviors from leaders and subversive strategies from followers. Hence the ambivalence of leader–follower relations.

The psychology of followers is in many ways more interesting than the psychology of leadership. Leaders and followers are engaged in an ongoing cost–benefit analysis. The leaders' calculations are pretty straightforward—they always intend to extract a larger share of resources from the interaction. Followers are not magnetically in thrall to leaders, as some writers would have it. Rather, they are constantly evaluating the relationship for its relative fairness; as soon as it appears that leaders are profiting disproportionately from the arrangement, followers will begin searching for exit strategies. The necessarily elaborate and intricate dance between leaders and followers accounts at least in part for the fascination of politics.

The point, however, is that in this model, leaders and followers are bound by calculations about relative self-interest. Leaders suggest it will be in the followers' best interest to follow them. Followers evaluate the benefits afforded by following various leaders, align themselves with the most beneficial option, and when that option is no longer beneficial, try to defect. In this model, it is essential to consider simultaneously the perspectives of both leaders and followers.

COMPETENCIES AS VIRTUES

Since the early 1980s, the practice of leadership selection and evaluation has been dominated by discussions of competencies (Boyatzis, 1982). Two new models, which frame competencies in terms of virtues, are quite interesting, and I briefly describe them next.

Emler's Moral Rules

The practice of management is fraught with moral problems. Consider a typical example. George Tenet was the Director of the Central Intelligence Agency (CIA) during the presidency of George W. Bush (2000–2004). In 2002 the Bush administration asked the CIA to provide evidence that the Iraqi government had weapons of mass destruction and the CIA complied. After the invasion of Iraq, no such weapons were found; facing public scrutiny, the Bush administration demanded that the CIA explain why it had provided such erroneous information. Clearly the CIA was being criticized to provide political cover for the Bush administration. As director, Tenet had two choices: He could defend his staff against the political assault coming from the White House, or he could join with the White House in criticizing his own staff. If he chose the former option, he would probably be fired; if he chose the latter option, he would alienate his staff. These are the difficult moral decisions that managers are faced with on a routine basis.

Why should we be interested in the moral competencies of managers? There are at least three reasons. First, as noted earlier, the single most important quality of leadership from the observers' perspective is integrity. Managers or leaders who are perceived as lacking integrity immediately lose their credibility and the respect of their staff. With no credibility or respect, such managers must rely entirely on position power—on giving orders and hoping that they will be followed. Second, from a pragmatic perspective, honesty is the best policy; it is very difficult to do business with people who ignore rules, violate legitimate expectations, and ignore their obligations and commitments. Moreover, it is as difficult to do business with corrupt governments and organizations as it is to work with dishonest managers. Finally, a manager's decisions can affect the well-being of everyone below him or her in the organizational hierarchy, and the more senior the manager, the more people will be influenced by his or her decisions. It is this magnification of consequences that makes managerial integrity so important.

Emler identified seven moral competencies needed by leaders, which he characterized as follows:

1. *The temptations of personal gain.* The higher a person's place in a hierarchy, the more discretion and freedom of action the person will enjoy. The first competency concerns not exploiting privileged access and control. As an example, I was elected president of a professional society a few years ago. The society had a semipermanent staff. At the planning meeting in the presidential suite the night before the annual conference began, the staff mentioned that it was customary for the president and the staff to have a banquet. I suggested that, if we were going to have a banquet paid for by the membership's money, then the membership should be invited to the banquet. The banquet was canceled, but the following year, with a new president, the banquets resumed. This is a trivial but quite common example of the first moral challenge of leadership.

2. *The temptations of tyranny.* Managers have more power than those who report to them. The second moral challenge concerns not using one's power to bully, harass, or intimidate others with less power. This injunction brings to mind the old adage that power corrupts and absolute power corrupts absolutely. It is, of course the essence of tyranny to bully the less powerful.

3. *The risks of failure.* Emler suggested that managers have a responsibility to ensure that their enterprises succeed. Dixon's (1991) book, *The Psychology of Military Incompetence,* recites in heart-rending detail the consequences that befall military personnel when their leaders make bad decisions. Similarly, some companies in some industries have dangerously lax safety procedures and they kill their employees. Emler suggested that the bad decisions that lead to organizational disasters are usually a predictable feature of the managers' past performance. As a corollary, he suggested that managers have a moral obligation to identify their blind spots and areas of incompetence so that they can guard against unnecessary mistakes. This supports Collins's (2002) finding that great CEOs are also humble, and therefore, willing to acknowledge shortcomings.

4. *Avoiding collateral damage.* Managers are not only responsible for protecting their staff from their mistakes, but many managerial de-

cisions have larger social consequences. Positive consequences should be pursued, negative consequences (even if they are unintended) should be avoided (if they are foreseeable). Managers should not promote products that are harmful, such as pharmaceuticals with excessive side effects, unsafe automobiles, buildings that collapse, or contaminated food products.

5. *Ensuring justice.* The concept of justice emerges from the practice of reciprocity and cooperation during games in childhood. Children (and adults) seem prewired to detect cheating and injustice— failures of reciprocity, sharing, turn-taking, and other unfair treatment. These tendencies become amplified and codified in the adult world. Perceptions of fairness are essentially judgments about justice. Managers should try to be even-handed and fair in the way they reward, criticize, sanction, praise their staff, and resolve disputes. Managers are, whether they want to be or not, in the role of Solomon, and if they play the role badly, it will be damaging to their staff.

6. *Pursuing a moral mandate.* Successful leaders promote a vision that explains, rationalizes, or justifies the activities of a group, team, or organization. People are attracted to or repelled by these visions, and some visions are more compelling than others. The visions themselves can be evaluated in terms of their moral content. "Greed is good" and "Enron will rip your face off" are examples of vision statements with less than attractive moral overtones. The point is that people usually join organizations because they have a view of what the organization stands for. Managers need to support that moral vision and not betray the workforce.

7. *Setting an example.* People are hard wired to imitate others, a capability that fosters child development. Most significant learning is social learning—imitating the behavior of models. Two factors principally determine the degree to which individuals are potent models: their status and the consequences to them of their behavior (cf. Bandura, 1963). It follows from this that managers are important role models for their staff, and the more senior the executive, the more powerfully he or she will function as a role model. Emler's last rule is that managers should be aware of their status as role models and behave accordingly.

Kaplan and Kaiser

Kaplan and Kaiser (2003a, 2003b) proposed an elegant model of leadership competencies that is organized in terms of seven ideas: three sets of two bipolar concepts and one meta-concept. The model begins by recognizing one of the oldest dichotomies in the history of leadership research, the distinction between structure and consideration (Fleishman, 1989), or between an autocratic use of power and a focus on the tasks at hand, and a democratic use of power and a concern for people (Leonard, 2003). Kaplan and Kaiser (2003b) referred to these two concepts as forceful and enabling: "Forceful leadership is about asserting one's own power, capability, and authority whereas enabling leadership is about creating conditions for others to lead and contribute" (p. 16).

The second theme that Kaplan and Kaiser highlighted is denoted by the terms *strategic* and *operational*. Strategic leadership involves developing, evaluating, selling, and revising "the big picture" and trying to understand, evaluate, and fine-tune business models, strategic marketing issues, and competitor analysis. Operational leadership concerns the efficient and effective implementation of strategic decisions. For example, Toyota has never worried about competitors discovering their manufacturing methods because they feel no one else can execute their methods as well as they can. Clearly, effective operational leadership can be a strategic competitive advantage.

Kaiser and Kaplan (2003a, 2003b) noted that, in prior work on concepts like forceful–enabling and strategic–operational, writers have maintained that each pair is conceptually orthogonal—that is, managers may use a forceful approach, an enabling approach, both approaches, or neither. Moreover, quantitative and qualitative reviews report strong positive correlations between ratings of forceful and enabling behaviors (Bass, 1990; Piccolo, Judge, & Ilies, 2003). However, Kaplan and Kaiser reported that senior managers routinely tend to be either forceful or enabling—just the opposite of what is suggested by previous research. In other words, most managers are overdeveloped on one side and underdeveloped on the other.

This leads to the third pair of bipolar concepts in this model, which concern performance, and are labeled overdoing and underdoing: "The idea is simply that when managers don't perform a function well, it is often because they either don't do enough of it or they do too much of it" (Kaplan & Kaiser, 2003b, p. 16). Thus, managers can be too forceful, or not forceful enough; they can be too enabling or not sufficiently enabling. Managers can be too strategic, or not strategic enough; they can also be too operational or not operational enough. As you can see, a combination of these three bipolar (but orthogonal) concepts leads to a surprisingly nuanced description of a manager's performance. Interestingly, when managerial performance is measured on a scale ranging from too little, to the right amount, to too much, the opposing behaviors (forceful–enabling, strategic–operational) are inversely related. According to Kaplan and Kaiser, this reflects the tendency for managers to be one-sided—relying too much on one approach and too little on the complementary approach.

The final concept in this deceptively simple model is versatility. This metaconcept informs the rest of the model. Versatility is an Aristotelian virtue, and it is defined as the ability to perform on both sides of both dualities (e.g., to be forceful or enabling, strategic or operational), as well as being able to judge correctly which approach is most appropriate for any given set of circumstances. Versatility is assumed to promote effectiveness. It is also rare. Kaplan and Kaiser reported that fewer than 20% of executives they studied are truly versatile as they defined the term. It is interesting to note that the percentage of executives who lack versatility is close to the upper bound estimate of the base rate for managerial incompetence.

It is important to mention two empirical observations regarding the Kaplan and Kaiser competency model. First, the standard rating methodology used to evaluate managers always assumes that more of anything positive is better, so that the more forceful a manager, the better the manager. The standard rating methodology for evaluating managers never includes a provision for a manager overdoing it, as Kaplan and Kaiser suggested should be done. Second, Kaplan and Kaiser devised a clever quantitative index of versatility—doing something to a degree that is proportionate to the problem at hand. This versatility index yields very substantial correlations ($r = .55–.68$) with ratings of managerial effectiveness.

SUMMARY

This chapter concerns personality and leadership. It makes several points that deserve to be highlighted. First, the fashionable distinction between managers and leaders is overdrawn; managers are, by definition, in leadership positions. It is also true that many managers need to improve their leadership skills, and there are natural leaders in every organization who are not in leadership roles. However, in principle, these issues can be resolved. They deserve close attention because the leadership capabilities of the management team dramatically impact the effectiveness of every organization.

A second point concerns the links between personality and leadership effectiveness. The conventional wisdom of I/O psychology since World War II is that such links do not exist. Actually, the conventional wisdom has been that personality is not related to occupational performance of any type (Ghiselli & Barthol, 1953; Guion & Gottier, 1965; Mischel, 1968). To the degree that opinions are shaped by data, the conventional wisdom on this topic should begin to change (cf. Judge et al., 2002). The data are quite clear that personality and leadership are closely connected—who you are determines how you lead—and the standard dimensions of normal personality are robust predictors of leadership effectiveness.

Although the conventional wisdom regarding the links between personality and occupational performance may have been wrong, personality psychologists have contributed to the confusion with their persistent internal squabbling and imprecise terminology. If we want to know about the links between personality and anything, we need to define our terms. It is important to distinguish between personality as evaluated by observers and personality as self-reported by actors. From the perspective of the observer, we now know that leaders must be perceived as having integrity, decisiveness, competence, vision, persistence, and humility. Whether or not they actually have these characteristics is not the issue; the point is that potential leaders must consistently act in ways that suggest they have these characteristics.

With regard to personality from the inside, what are the self-reported or internal characteristics that leaders must actually possess to be effective? The internal characteristics of leaders can be summarized as competencies, or in the language of Emler, Kaplan, and Kaiser, as virtues. The work of Kaplan and Kaiser (2003a, 2003b) and Emler (2003) suggest that lists of competencies converge on a small number of themes—maintaining self-control, treating others with respect, building and maintaining a team, and exerting control over others to the right degree, in the right amount, at the right time. It is a relatively trivial task to translate competencies into the language of personality, and well-validated measures of personality predict competency ratings with a level of accuracy that rivals the best psychometric predictions available anywhere. Thus, the competency movement has had the welcome consequence of legitimizing personality concepts in the culture of the modern organization.

4

Lives in Public: Personality and Team Performance

Humans evolved as group-living animals and they are inherently social. That is, people need social interaction on a constant basis to avoid feeling lonely and ignored, but they also need to be part of a group for their long-term physical survival. Not surprisingly, then, the most significant human achievements are the result of groups working together to complete projects. Despite this historical record of collective human accomplishment, theoretical perspectives in psychology are typically versions of individualism—they describe people as selfish, self-centered, and primarily motivated by needs for self-development and self-advancement (cf. Hogan, 1975). Despite the pervasiveness and popularity of this individualistic perspective, it is simply inconsistent with the facts of human evolution and history.

In contrast with mainstream psychology, sociologists focus on collective (or group) phenomena and see individualism as a symptom of a decadent society—sociologists believe that individualism only emerges in societies that have lost their vitality and emotional appeal. The sociological critique of individualism is more consistent with human evolutionary history than the psychological view. Although people are often absorbed by their interior lives, the consequential parts of their lives are conducted in public, with other people, as they try to get along and get ahead. This chapter concerns lives in public; it reviews the psychology of groups and teams, paying special attention to the links between individual personality and group and team performance.

The word *team* is standard parlance in business today. The word is used to designate any group that pursues a shared goal. There is even a team-related verb in common usage, *to team with,* as in "We teamed with Agency Q to complete this project." Consequently, in everyday language the word *team* has become nearly indistinguishable from the concept of a work group. Nonetheless, it seems sensible (if perhaps futile) to distinguish a team from a work group. Although a team can be a work group, a work group is not necessarily a team.

Teams are often defined as "two or more people who ... ." There are two-person teams—for example, tennis or squash doubles teams— but there are qualitative differences between two-person teams (dyads) and three-person teams (triads). Because two people can usually negotiate a *modus vivendi,* dyads are relatively easy to establish and maintain. Even when there is conflict within a dyad, differences can usually be resolved if one person can deal maturely with conflict. Triads, however, are inherently more complex and unstable than two-person groups. When three people interact, the outcome is much harder to predict—because with three people interacting, coalitions often form in which two people gang up on the third. Obviously, dyadic and triadic relationships evolve, overlap, and interact in relation to the size of the work group. If one watches carefully, one will see that all larger groups break down into singles, dyads, and triads. Groups of five will behave as a dyad–triad combination or two dyads and a singleton, the latter a potential coalition target.

A team should be defined as three or more people (a) who work toward a common goal; (b) whose performance is interdependent (i.e., what one person does depends on what the others do), (c) who share common leadership, (d) who share a common fate that depends on the performance of the team, and (e) who see themselves as being part of a team with a common goal and a shared fate. This definition is somewhat different from the traditional account in two ways. First, this definition treats dyads as a special case and not as true teams, and it does so because the dynamics of a dyad are so much simpler than those of a triad. Second, the definition emphasizes phenomenology: People are only members of a team if they see themselves as members, if they participate to some degree in a "shared mental model"

(Klimoski & Mohammed, 1994). It should be obvious that a team is a special kind of a group; it is a task-oriented group with reasonably well-defined roles. Nonetheless, no matter how valid and correct this definition of a team may be, people will continue to use the word *team* to refer to any group of people who work together.

Finally, it is important not to reify the concept of a team; teams are composed of individuals, and it is the characteristics of those individuals that contribute to and define the performance of the team (in ways that are often hard to predict). People are nested in teams, and teams are nested in organizations. Teams do not behave, people do, and in so doing, they create team-level phenomena (cf. Koslowski & Bell, 2003, p. 335).

HISTORY OF TEAMS

Most people learn about teams through participation in athletic games during their school years. Many occupations in adulthood require teamwork: football, emergency response teams, symphony orchestras, movie production companies, space missions, construction sites, and so on. Taking part in a team also gives people a sense of identity; it helps define who they are. Being a member of a team very often means something important is at stake. Moreover, to become a member of many real teams involves a long, competitive process before one is accepted. Teams are everywhere in modern occupational life, and some people earn their living by providing team-building services to organizations.

Academics have historically studied teams from a detached, basic science perspective, by asking about the laws of team formation and group dynamics; that is, they have studied teams for their own sake, with no particular agenda or goal in mind. Business would be interested in teams only if there is a payoff; for example, if there are consequences associated with different forms of team management. Because the business perspective is more concerned with consequences, I adopt it here. There seem to be four related historical sources for the modern business interest in teams: sociotechnical systems, humanistic psychology, the American quality movement, and the downsizing movement aimed at reducing middle management.

Sociotechnical Systems

The teaming movement rests on the view that, if teams can be established and maintained, positive organizational outcomes will emerge.

Sociotechnical systems (Cherns, 1976) began with the reverse insight—namely, that when established teams fall apart, an organization will then experience lower productivity, lower morale, and other negative consequences. A seminal paper by Trist and Bamforth (1951) described the consequences of replacing group-based mining methods with mechanized mining equipment. The group-based method involved local supervision, self-selection into tasks, control over planning and scheduling, multitasking, and autonomous local control of the work. With the implementation of mechanized mining, the previous social structure was destroyed, and a wide range of individual, organizational, and performance problems ensued.

Humanistic Psychology

Maslow popularized humanistic psychology after World War II. Maslow, a Marxist from the 1930s, believed that the proper goal of the state is to help each citizen develop his or her potential to the maximum. Consistent with this belief, he proposed a theory of motivation in which the highest motive is a need for self-actualization, a drive to fulfill one's latent potentialities (which humane organizations respect). A corollary of this assumption is that bad things happen to people when this motive is frustrated. There are four points to be noted about Maslow's concept of self-actualization. First, it is an element of Marxist ideology, an economic perspective that has been largely discredited on the world historical stage. Second, the concept of self-actualization, which is actually pretty hard to define, makes no sense in evolutionary terms, except as an excuse for selfishness. For a concept to qualify as a human motive, it needs to be interpretable in terms of what we know about natural selection. No reputable ethologist uses the concept of self-actualization to understand the behavior of seagulls or the higher primates. Third, despite over 50 years of research on the topic of self-actualization, no one has yet devised a way to measure individual differences in the construct. This strongly raises the suspicion that it does not exist. Fourth, despite the obvious problems with the concept of self-actualization, it is the favorite motivational theory of organizational psychologists. Sometimes it is called self-actualization, sometimes it is called intrinsic motivation (Herzberg, 1966), and sometimes it is called internal motivation (Hackman & Oldham, 1976). A key feature of this vastly popular motivational theory is that the motive itself is ineffable, incapable of being reduced to anything more physiologically primitive, but when it is frustrated, people allegedly suffer.

The 1960s began a period of dramatic cultural upheaval in the United States that included massive public demonstrations in favor of civil rights and against the U.S. military invasion of Vietnam. At the same time, a curious complacency about work came into being. Smart applied psychologists wrote books on what they perceived to be as a looming crisis—namely, how to deal with leisure time in the postindustrial society! Hackman and Oldham were concerned about an emerging crisis in the labor force, employee alienation. They argued that people were no longer happy merely to have a job; they needed to be engaged in their work and find it personally meaningful and self-enhancing (as if working for a salary could ever serve those functions for any extended period of time). The bottom line was this: In the 1970s, business managers spent a great deal of time and energy worrying about how to put workers into teams to create a more meaningful (i.e., motivating in Maslow's terms) working environment for them.

The American Quality Movement

The Japanese economic miracle after World War II impressed U.S. business. What was the secret of the ability of Japanese manufacturing to penetrate Western markets in the 1960s and 1970s? For many people, the answer was total quality management (TQM), a Japanese management practice that evolved after World War II. TQM is inherently hostile to personality; it is based on the assumption that individual differences in worker characteristics are relatively trivial influences on work process outcomes. Workers are "special causes" of errors in a system—they are replaceable cogs in a work process that account for perhaps 10% of the variance in team performance. Most of the variance in work process outcomes is due to "common causes"—flaws in the design of the system (Deming, 1986). Managers use statistical process controls (SPCs) to track variations in team performance. They establish a baseline work outcome measure and set allowable tolerances around the baseline. Special causes show up as spikes in an SPC chart and they are typically ignored—they are error variance. If the organization can learn to manage common causes, the outcome measures will remain within the desired tolerances.

The TQM model is widely accepted in the United States, but there is little empirical support for the many practices that stem from it. With the exception of jobs such as machine operators, common causes do not influence work outcomes to the extent TQM advocates propose (Cascio,

1998). Popular TQM practices include continuous process improvement, six sigma, Kaizen methods, just-in-time management, and quality
circles—a special kind of team devoted to improving the performance
of other teams. In quality circles, employees meet regularly to discuss
problems in the work group; these meetings are intended to improve
the quality and productivity of manufacturing and to reduce costs, pre-
sumably by helping employees see their work as more meaningful
(Maslow's motive).

Western firms began using quality circles in the 1970s; by 1990, two
thirds of the *Fortune* 1000 firms reported using them (Lawler,
Mohrman, & Ledford, 1992). Early research indicated that quality circles sometimes improved organizational performance. A consulting
bandwagon quickly formed, based on the belief that, if quality circles
work in the factory, they will work everywhere in the workplace. Although quality circles do not really fit administrative and service jobs,
the word *team* carries such a positive emotional tone that the concept is
difficult to resist. Consultants and human resource specialists were
hired to make individualistic corporate cultures team oriented. By the
mid-1990s, the use of quality circles began to decline for three reasons.
First, their use seemed not to affect employee satisfaction. Second, they
tended not to persist over time because of the intragroup tensions that
are created by the process of constant criticism. Third, the willingness to
participate in a quality circle is an individual differences phenomenon
(i.e., a function of personality), not a generally shared disposition.
Again, the widespread enthusiasm for quality circles was created by an
effort to improve business practices and slow the movement of
Japanese manufactured products into Western markets.

Teams as a Consequence of Downsizing

In the late 1970s, the world economy began moving toward a reces-
sion, and businesses everywhere began to consider restructuring and
downsizing as a way of controlling costs and increasing productivity.
In the 1980s and early 1990s, between one third and one half of all me-
dium and large firms in North America and Western Europe down-
sized, and two thirds of those companies did so more than once.
Downsizing became a hot topic in management circles. The essence of
downsizing was a desire to reduce costs, principally by terminating the
employment of people thought to be unproductive, unnecessary, or
redundant. Because managers are paid more than hourly employees,

costs could be reduced more rapidly by firing managers than hourly employees. This logic leads inexorably to the concept of self-managed work groups. A self-managed team not only brings all the advantages that accrue to teaming, but it does so without the cost of a manager. The fourth historical factor driving the importance of teams to organizations was the desire to reduce personnel costs, especially the cost of middle managers.

SOCIOANALYTIC THEORY AS ROLE THEORY

Chapter 1 outlines socioanalytic theory (Hogan, 2004), a model of personality designed to explain individual differences in career success; that is, individual differences in significant organizational behavior. Socioanalytic theory argues that people are primarily motivated by needs for acceptance and approval, for status and power, and for meaning and purpose (alternatively, they are motivated by the fear of losing these things). It further argues that these needs are fulfilled during social interaction, typically at work. Finally, it suggests that there are specific structural requirements for interactions to be possible: Interactions depend on the agenda for an interaction, and roles for the actors to play. Outside of our roles, we have little to say to one another.

In private life, we make up our agendas (Let's get together and have a drink) and our roles (the made-up role is the person that you think you are—your identity). At work, however, the organization sets the agendas (Let's meet and figure out how to solve this problem) and assigns the roles (chief financial officer, account manager, etc.). If we know the agenda for an interaction and the roles that the other people occupy, we then understand how the other persons in the interaction will behave, and what their expectations will be regarding our behavior. Part of what it means to be inherently sociable is to be responsive to others' expectations and respect their wishes.

People who occupy the same roles do not perform them in the same way, although many sociologists believe they will. The manner in which people play their roles depends on their identity, their own view of who they are. A college lecture is a kind of organizational interaction. In a typical lecture, there are two roles: the professor and the student. Professors approach the role of lecturer in different ways, and students try to play the role of student so as to highlight their individuality and send the other students a message about who they really are, and to tell the professor how they want to be regarded. Role performance is therefore strongly influenced by personal identity. The larger point, once again, is that people are linked to teams through the roles that they have as team members, but there are important, personality-based individual differences in how people play the same role.

There are actually two kinds of roles in a work group or organization. There are formal roles—sales rep, customer service manager, and so on. But there are also psychological roles that need to be filled for a group to operate effectively. These include an emergent leader who organizes work, manages disputes, and tries to provide direction—a task leader. There should also be someone who attends to the morale of the group—a socioemotional leader. Someone needs to be able to find solutions to problems that inevitably arise, and someone needs to be a master at arms or sheriff who attends to issues of law and order. The topic of psychological roles is discussed in more detail later in this chapter. The point that I am trying to make here is that roles—both formal and psychological—entail certain performance requirements; because of their talent and personalities, some people are better suited to perform certain roles than others.

Some people are shy and deferential; others are outgoing and bold. Some people are anxious and self-doubting; others are confident and stress resistant. Some people are tough and insensitive; others are caring and sensitive. Some people are impulsive and disorganized; others are planful and self-disciplined. Some people are literal-minded, concrete thinkers; others are imaginative and speculative. They are this way by virtue of their innate temperament and various life experiences, and they are consistently this way, over extended periods of time. The foregoing is a highly abbreviated account of the Big Five model of personality structure (Wiggins, 1996). The point, however, is that (a) roles differ in the characteristics required to perform them well, and (b) people differ in the characteristics that they bring to roles, so that (c) some people are better suited to fill certain roles than others.

The reader may regard the foregoing as blindingly obvious, but standard sociological role theory (Goffman, 1959) regards people as essentially fungible, so that any single person can fill just about any role. Moreover, for sociologists, it is the experience of being in a role that creates a person's identity. The way people think about themselves (their identities) is shaped and influenced by their experience in various occupational roles. However, people also bring characteristic qualities to their roles, and people in the same roles perform them differently. Moreover, awareness of the fact that some people are better suited for some roles than others is not widely shared. Organizations routinely assign people to roles with no consideration for their personality. Thus, they put people who are shy and retiring into sales roles, they put people who are tough and insensitive into customer service roles, and they put people who are impulsive and easily bored into jobs that require vigilance and attention to detail (e.g., long-distance truck drivers). More important for this discussion, these considerations are crucial for understanding how to staff a team.

PERSONALITY, GROUP, AND TEAM EFFECTIVENESS

If we assume that certain people will perform more effectively in certain team roles than others, then we should be able to compose teams in a rational manner. The notion that personality can influence team performance has come up repeatedly in the group dynamics literature over the years. For example, Golembiewski (1962) suggested that personality characteristics are as important as group properties for understanding group behavior. Steiner (1972) argued that team composition must influence team performance, but that there was not much data to support his view. Hackman and Morris (1975) noted that personality may have both positive (enhancing and facilitative) and negative (detrimental and degrading) effects on group performance. Shaw (1976) suggested that individual-level emotional stability and emotional control positively influence, and depression, anxiety and paranoia negatively influence, group-level effectiveness, cohesion, morale, and efficient communication. Ridgeway (1983) argued that group effectiveness "emerges from the interaction of skills and personalities of the members, the nature of the task, the groups' structure and norms, and the influence of the outside environment" (p. 281). Finally, Koslowski and Bell (2003) observed that "personality composition has important implications for team effectiveness" (p. 339).

These claims are commonsensical but the empirical literature supports them only ambiguously. Mann (1959) noted that the relation between personality and team performance had been studied extensively for 50 years, but the research led to few firm conclusions. Almost 40 years later, Kahan, Webb, Shavelson, and Stolzenberg (1985) concluded that "It does not appear promising at the present time to use personality measures in determining group composition" (p. 28). There seems to be a major mismatch between what people generally believe and what is empirically supported.

It is important to distinguish between the determinants of group behavior in general and the determinants of group effectiveness in particular. Social psychologists have studied the behavior of people in groups since the end of the 19th century, but this research is a catalog of facts with no organizing theme. About 1990, industrial psychologists began studying groups (Levine & Moreland, 1990); they turned the focus from group behavior to group effectiveness. This focus is heartily to be endorsed, along with Koslowski and Bell (2003).

One reason the findings regarding personality and group performance have been so inconsistent lies in the fact that early research largely ignored the role of the task in determining group performance. Morris (1966) pointed out that most prior research on personality and group performance ignored the group's task. Hackman and Morris (1975) suggested that it is almost useless to try to predict group performance without specifying the group's task. They also noted that no fully satisfactory method for classifying group tasks has yet been developed—and I return to this problem shortly. A second reason these findings have been so inconsistent is that, earlier on, there was no accepted taxonomy of personality variables. The lack of a taxonomy made it nearly impossible to compare results across studies. With the widespread acceptance of the Big Five model (Wiggins, 1996), such comparisons are now possible.

There is a relatively well-accepted meta-theoretical model for thinking about team effectiveness (cf. Ridgeway, 1983; Steiner, 1972). This model, presented in Figure 4.1, illustrates the relation among input factors, group interaction process, and group performance outcomes. Implicit in Figure 4.1 are several empirical questions about group performance—for example, how input factors affect group processes, how group processes interact and then impact group performance, and how input factors influence group performance.

Personality affects group performance both as an input variable and as a factor impacting team processes, and it is important to distinguish these two kinds of effects. One can make predictions about a team composed of ambitious (i.e., energetic and hard-working) people based on what one knows about ambitious people, or one can make predictions based on how trait similarity impacts team performance, where the trait in this case is ambition. Haythorn's (1968) classic review concerns the second issue; I am concerned with the first.

Following Hackman and Morris (1975), we can trace the effects of personality as an input factor through its impact on three mediating

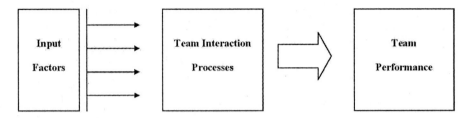

Fig. 4.1 Metatheoretical model of team effectiveness.

variables (part of the process in Figure 4.1) that link input factors with performance measures. These mediating variables include:

1. The effort group members exert on a task.
2. The knowledge and skills group members can apply to a task.
3. The task performance strategies used to accomplish a task.

Each of these mediating variables is complex. For example, the effort a team applies to a task is a function of individual characteristics, group norms, task reward system, and process variables such as communication structure. Nonetheless, personality will impact these mediating variables. For example, with regard to effort, persons with high scores on the HPI (Hogan & Hogan, 2002a) scales for Ambition and Prudence are hard working, achievement oriented, and persistent. With regard to knowledge and skills, persons with high scores on the HPI Learning Style scale are curious, open-minded, and motivated to stay up to date with new developments in their field. Similarly, with regard to task performance strategies, persons with high scores on the HPI Intellectance scale approach tasks in an analytic and strategic manner.

Over the past 10 years, research has begun to accumulate bearing on the impact of personality on team performance. In a very interesting paper, LePine, Hollenbeck, Ilgen, and Hedlund (1997) studied 51 four-person teams performing a computerized decision-making task. Performance was defined in terms of the match between the team's decision and the correct decision as defined by the rules of the simulation. The analyses concerned the degree to which the intelligence and conscientiousness of the team leader, and of the team, influenced the performance of the team. Results showed that the intelligence of either the leader or the staff alone was unrelated to team performance; rather, performance was a function of both the leader and the staff having high scores on intelligence. Similarly, the conscientiousness of the leader or the staff alone was unrelated to team performance; again, team performance was a function of both the leader and the staff having high scores for conscientiousness. As the authors noted,

> [O]ur results are consistent with the popular cliché regarding teams: A chain is only as strong as its weakest link ... . When the staff's weakest member had relative high g and conscientiousness, the team performed well but only when the leader was also high in g and conscientiousness. A poor leader ... neutralized the effect of a good staff (and vice versa). (p. 807)

Additional analyses revealed that the team's reaction to the weakest member depended on whether that member was low on g or conscientiousness: The team helped low-g members but ignored low-conscientiousness members.

In a related and equally important piece of team research, Barrick, Stewart, and Neubert (1998) studied 252 people in 22 teams that assemble small appliances, 285 people in 19 teams that assemble electronic equipment, 103 people from 6 fabrication and maintenance teams in one rubber-manufacturing plant and 52 people from 8 fabrication and maintenance teams in a second rubber-manufacturing plant. The research used a measure of cognitive ability and FFM measure of personality to predict team performance, and team performance was defined in terms of supervisors' ratings. This study is particularly strong from a methodological perspective, and the key findings can be summarized as follows. First, teams with higher average levels of cognitive ability had higher rated performance. Second, teams with higher average levels of conscientiousness, agreeableness, and emotional stability had higher rated performance. Third, teams with higher average levels of extroversion and emotional stability were more viable over the long term. Fourth, teams with no very low-conscientiousness members report less conflict, more communication, and more workload sharing. Fifth, teams containing one person with a very low score for agreeableness, extroversion, or emotional stability had lower performance, less cohesion, more conflict, less open communications, and less workload sharing.

The authors suggested two practical implications for their study, with which I strongly agree. First, selecting team members with higher levels of cognitive ability, conscientiousness, agreeableness, and emotional stability will enhance team performance. Second, although agreeableness and emotional stability do not predict individual job performance as well as cognitive ability and conscientiousness, when aggregated, they are important predictors of team performance.

The last study I review replicates and extends these earlier findings. Neuman and Wright (1999) studied 79 four-person work teams that were structured to maximize team member interaction and interdependence. These teams processed claims for compensation and vacation benefits. Poor performance in this area had caused major problems for the organization earlier, and the team approach was implemented to fix the problem. All team members completed a measure of cognitive ability and an FFM personality inventory. The criteria consisted of peer ratings of individual performance; three supervisors rated the performance of each team. Cognitive ability, agreeableness, and conscientiousness predicted individual performance ratings, and both predicted performance beyond that predicted by cognitive ability. At the team level, cognitive ability, agreeableness, and conscientiousness predicted supervisors' ratings of team performance, with personality significantly increasing predictive power over that provided by cognitive ability.

I conclude this discussion of personality and team effectiveness with three observations. First, the data clearly indicate that personality predicts team performance both at the individual and the team level, and it adds variance to that predicted by cognitive ability. The aspects of personality that predict team performance depend on the team task, but personality is a stable predictor of team performance.

Second, the data clearly indicate that three personality variables—emotional stability, agreeableness, and conscientiousness—are essential components of team performance. People with low scores on measures of each of these three constructs behave differently—low emotional stability leads to moodiness, low agreeableness leads to irritability, and low conscientiousness leads to carelessness—but the consequences of their behavior are all the same. People with low scores on emotional stability, agreeableness, and conscientiousness are not rewarding to deal with; as a result, they are disruptive team members. At stake here is an important generalization about teams. Effective teams depend on the members being good team players. The data clearly suggest the profile of a good team player: high scores on measures of emotional stability, agreeableness, and conscientiousness.

Third, as Neuman and Wright (1999) noted, these studies "emphasize the importance of team composition. Team selection requires attention to the appropriate mix of team members for task and team performance" (p. 386). I turn now to precisely that topic: how to compose effective teams.

COMPOSING EFFECTIVE WORK GROUPS

There is an old literature suggesting that certain personality types are an essential component of effective team functioning.

Belbin

Belbin (1981) developed an interesting and intuitive model for composing effective teams that is popular in the United Kingdom, but rarely mentioned by writers in the United States. Over a period of 9 years, Belbin watched teams of managers playing management games, and the performance of the team was measured in terms of winning or losing the game. Belbin drew a distinction between what he called functional roles and team roles. A person's functional role is defined by his or her job title. A person's team role (which I referred to earlier as an informal role) is defined by what he or she actually does while the team is performing. A person who is naturally imaginative might migrate to a team or informal role of problem solver, whereas a compulsive person might migrate to an informal role of one who tidies up loose ends.

Three points about Belbin's model should be emphasized. First, he suggested that people migrate to informal team roles based on their personalities; certain personality styles make people a natural fit with certain informal team roles. Second, Belbin identified nine team or informal roles, presented in Table 4.1. Table 4.1 defines the roles, describes the personality style associated with each role, and then describes the characteristic personal shortcomings associated with each role.

The third and most important point about Belbin's model concerns his concept of team role balance. He maintained that in effective teams, each role is filled appropriately. That is, "there is a cause and effect relationship between team role balance and team performance" (Senior, 1997, p. 246). So, for Belbin, personality impacts team performance through the roles required for effective team performance. An effective team contains nine informal team roles, and there is a characteristic personality style associated with each role. Dulewicz (1995) and Senior (1997) provided empirical support for Belbin's model.

In summary, Belbin's focus on the fit between personal style and informal team roles is important for understanding how personality affects team performance. I think that Belbin is correct in his general

Table 4.1

Belbin's Taxonomy of Team Roles

Role	Features	Positive Qualities	Allowable Weakness	Contribution
Chairman	Calm, controlled, self-confident	Evaluates contributions on their merits—task oriented, not prejudiced	Average intelligence and creativity	• Clarifies goals • Identifies problems, establishes priorities • Defines roles • Summarizes feelings of the group
Shaper	High-strung and dynamic	Energetic, willing to challenge group's performance	Irritable and impatient	• Identifies roles, tasks, and responsibilities • Pushes group for performance
Creative thinker	Individualistic and unorthodox	Bright and imaginative	Impractical and disorganized	• Generates ideas • Generates solutions • Criticizes current actions
Evaluator	Sober and unemotional	Discrete and hard-headed	No leadership ability	• Analyzes problems • Clarifies issues • Evaluates others' contributions
Negotiator	Extroverted, curious, communicative	Ability to build relationships	Easily bored	• Brings in ideas from the outside
Team worker	Pleasant but mild	Responsiveness to people, promotes team spirit	Indecisive in crisis	• Emphasizes task completion • Promoting sense of urgency • Finding errors
Company Worker	Conservative and predictable	Organized, disciplined, hard-working	Inflexible, resistant to change	• Focus • Planning
Finisher	Orderly, conscientious, and anxious	Perfectionism	Worried about small things	• Supportive and helping others • Building on others' ideas

orientation—that a mixture of types of people is necessary for the effective functioning of teams—but he is not specific regarding which types are needed and when. Moreover, his measurement model is poorly validated, and his taxonomy of team roles is rather arbitrary. For a somewhat more rigorous taxonomy of teams and team roles, we need to turn to another researcher, John Holland.

Holland

Because the major determinant of team behavior is the team task (Hackman & Morris, 1975), a taxonomy of teams could be based on a taxonomy of team tasks. I propose classifying team tasks according to the behaviors or activities required of members to complete them—in McGrath's (1984) terms, according to the tasks as a set of behavioral requirements for team performance. Doing this results in six team task categories, presented in Table 4.2. A number of earlier writers have classified team tasks in this way. For example, McCormick, Finn, and Scheirs (1957), analyzing job requirements, needed only seven factors to characterize the 4,000 jobs listed in the *Dictionary of Occupational Titles* at that time. The most developed of these typologies were presented by McGrath (1984) and Holland (1986). I prefer the Holland model because it provides explicit links between task preferences and personality.

Holland defined six ideal occupational types, which he called realistic, investigative, artistic, social, enterprising, and conventional. Each of these occupational types is also a personality type with distinctive characteristics. Typical realistic occupations include information technology, law enforcement, the military, and professional athletics; typical realistic tasks include building, operating, and maintaining equipment, and other practical tasks that often require mechanical dexterity and physical courage. Investigative occupations include all forms of scientific research; typical investigative tasks include researching and designing systems, problem identification, and problem solving. Artistic occupations include art, music, literature, philosophy, architecture, and landscaping; typical artistic tasks include designing and creating products and entertaining people. Social occupations include teaching, medicine, social work, human resources, and librarianship; typical social tasks involve helping and teaching other people, and operating emergency response teams. Enterprising occupations include sales, politics, and entrepreneurship; typical entrepreneurial tasks involve persuading, manipulating, and coopting other people. Conventional

Table 4.2

Task Classification

| | Tasks | | | | | |
	Mechanical/ Technical	Intellectual/ Analytic	Imaginative/ Aesthetic	Social	Manipulative/ Persuasive	Logical/ Precision
Descriptors	Construction, operation, maintenance of things	Generation, exploration, or verification of knowledge	Invention, arrangement, or production of expressive products	Training, assisting, or serving others	Organization, motivation, or persuasion of others	Performance of explicit, routine, or tasks requiring attention to detail
Cognates						
Guilford, Christensen, Bond, and Sutton (1954)	Mechanical	Scientific	Aesthetic	Social	Business	Clerical
McCormick, Finn, and Scheirs (1957)	Manual	Mental	Artistic	Personal contact	—	Precision
McGrath (1984)	Performances/ contests (execution)	Planning/ decision making	Creativity	—	Cognitive conflict/mixed motive (negotiation)	Intellective
Holland (1986)	Realistic	Intellectual	Artistic	Social	Enterprising	Conventional

occupations include insurance, accounting, tax law, finance, and most office work; typical conventional tasks involve monitoring systems, counting things, organizing papers, regulating processes or people, and many law enforcement activities.

Realistic types, in personality terms, are robust, tough, conforming, and action oriented. Investigative types are cerebral, analytical, somewhat introverted, and enjoy challenging authority. Artistic types are imaginative, nonconforming, and entertaining. Social types are altruistic, helpful, and sympathetic. Enterprising types are aggressive, bold, and outgoing. Conventional types are conforming, procedural, orderly, and detail oriented.

If we know what tasks are required to do a job, then we can classify that job according to the Holland model, and we know about the personality characteristics needed to perform it. Similarly, if we know what the main tasks for a work group are, we can then use the same system to classify a work group and then staff it with the relevant personality types. Using an extensive list of team tasks from the U.S. Navy, Hogan, Driskell, and Raza (1988) demonstrated that (a) tasks can be classified with excellent reliability using this system, and (b) the system was comprehensive—no tasks were leftover. My point here is that the Holland model provides a simple, reliable, and exhaustive way to classify team tasks, and therefore to classify teams. More important, this classification method leads to a number of useful insights about personality and team performance. I mention three.

First, the Holland model provides a useful way to think about what happens to work groups when their tasks change. Many occupational tasks are realistic and conventional—they involve watch standing, completing forms, ordering supplies, maintaining equipment and schedules, checking accuracy, organizing materials, transacting with customers, assembling simple components, and meter monitoring. These jobs require vigilance, focus, attention to detail, and careful adherence to procedure most of the time. Think abut standing a sonar watch on a ship. A technician watches a scope carefully, searching areas according to a schedule, while maintaining the equipment and keeping logs. What happens when the sonar watch gets real, when an unidentified contact is discovered? The realistic and conventional task turns into an investigative and artistic task—a problem-solving task as the operator tries to classify the contact as a fish or enemy submarine. The requirements of a problem-solving task are vastly different from the requirements of a watch-standing task: People must do things in unusual and nonstandard ways, think and act outside the dots, adapt, improvise, and innovate. This suggests that those persons who are best suited for watch standing are worst suited for problem solving, that persons who are well-suited for the peacetime military will be poorly suited for the wartime military and vice versa. Recognizing that the nature of the team task can change suddenly suggests that managers should create special subgroups whose talent and personality are suited for "red-alert" conditions.

A second insight from the Holland model concerns the fact that, in the Holland hexagon, the axis running from artistic to conventional occupations is one of nonconformity to conformity, and the axis running from the top to the bottom of the Holland hexagon is one of introversion to extroversion (see Figure 4.2). A good member of a realistic and conventional team should be introverted and conscientious, whereas a good member of an investigative and artistic team should be introverted and nonconforming. A good teacher, health care professional, or cleric should be extroverted and nonconforming, whereas a good lawyer, financier, or business executive should be extroverted and conforming. Thus, Holland's model extends Belbin's suggestions about using personality to compose work groups by specifying the

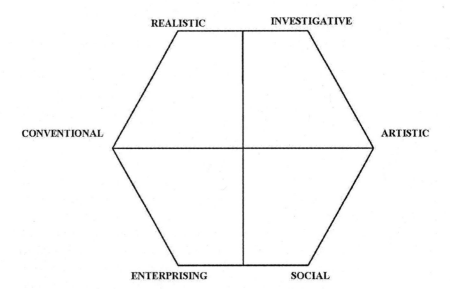

Fig. 4.2   The Holland model of vocational types.

personality characteristics needed for optimal performance for a particular team task.

Third, and most important, people often say leadership depends on the situation. But how does leadership depend on the situation? Recall the model of leadership that comes from the Ohio State leadership research after World War II. The argument had two parts. The first was that there are two prototypical or megadimensions underlying leadership. One dimension concerns providing group members with structure (e.g., time lines, rules, limits, and direction); the second dimension concerns providing them with consideration (e.g., attention, pats on the back, concern about their welfare, clean work environment, etc.). The second part of the argument is that competent managers provide their staff with equal amounts of structure and consideration. However, the Ohio State research was done at a manufacturing plant that built tractors. Building tractors is, in Holland's terms, a realistic job. Structure and consideration are important, but not in the way the Ohio State studies have been interpreted.

More recent data suggest that structure is more important for realistic and conventional task groups (football teams, fire departments). Members of these groups want to know what is wanted, when it is wanted, how they will be evaluated, and how they will be paid; more important, they get angry if their manager tries to involve them in participatory management because they are minimally interested in consideration. On the other hand, members of enterprising and social groups (teachers, airline flight attendants) want lots of consideration and get angry if managers try to impose structure on them because they will see that as dictatorial. The conclusion is that structure matters more to realistic and conventional work groups, and consideration matters more to enterprising and social ones. This suggests, then, that managers and leaders should spend their time differently with these groups.

Realistic, conventional, enterprising, and social tasks comprise the bulk of the jobs in the economy. The remaining two Holland types—investigative and artistic—are a small fraction of the workforce. Investigative and artistic work teams specialize in creative problem solving. What is the best way to manage investigative or artistic teams whose primary tasks concern innovation? No one really knows, although Mumford (2004) provided a useful review. Although the future of our civilization depends on innovation and creativity, psychologists have contributed only marginally toward answering the question of how to manage creative talent. For the most part, investigative or artistic people, such as designers, writers, musicians, criminal investigators, political philosophers, and scientific researchers, are solitary workers who occasionally participate in interdisciplinary groups. To manage an artistic or investigative team, a leader will have to pay extra attention to building individual relationships with individual team members and gradually merge the relationships into a larger group. It may be helpful to remind the group of the important functions managers serve (acquiring resources and preserving the status of the group). It is also useful to remind managers that creative people may need to be "project floaters" rather than long-serving group members.

Personality and Team Culture

Culture is about values, and values are important determinants of behavior. Values form the core of individual identity; in addition, they tell us what we enjoy doing, and they tell us about the kinds of people with whom we enjoy working and interacting. We prefer to work with, and we like, others who share our values. The fact that they share our values makes their behavior more predictable, but perhaps more important, the fact that they share our values means that they approve of us. Conversely, we dislike and tend to avoid people who hold different values, in part because it is harder to predict their behavior, and in part because, by not sharing our values, they implicitly criticize us.

This model also has important implications for occupational psychology. Holland (1986) and Super (1957) argued that people select, and are most happy with, occupations and careers that are congruent with their self-concept (where self-concept is synonymous with their values). Empirical results overwhelmingly support their views.

The major problem with research evaluating the fit between individuals and team culture concerns how to match the units of assessment—people are profiled using personality measures, cultures are profiled using different metrics. Rousseau (1990) suggested people and cultures can be compared using a framework that includes fundamental assumptions, behavioral norms and expectations, and values. Values are the elements around which norms, symbols, rituals, and other group activities are organized. As O'Reilly, Chatman, and Caldwell (1991) noted, "values in organizational culture are fundamentally linked to the psychological process of identity formation in which individuals ... seek a social identity that provides meaning and connectedness" (p. 492). O'Reilly et al. provided an empirical test of the view that the congruence between a person's values and the culture where he or she works improves individual performance. They developed a 54-item Q-sort set, with items reflecting such values as innovation, stability, and security. Individuals described themselves with the items, creating a Q-sort profile, then they used the items to describe the culture of the organization where they worked, creating another Q-sort profile. The two profiles were correlated, creating an index of person–culture fit. They found that the greater the fit, the more job satisfaction and organizational commitment 1 year later, and the less turnover 2 years later.

The main point of this section is that personality affects team performance in two ways: in terms of how an individual's interpersonal style impacts the other members of a team and in terms of how an individual's values fit with the culture of the team, where culture is defined in terms of the aggregated values of the team.

Team Building

Tuckman (1965) reviewed the literature from group therapy, T-groups, and natural and laboratory studies of team performance, and proposed that teams emerge and develop through four developmental stages. The model has real verisimilitude—it fits with my experience. In addition, Koslowski and Bell (2003) noted that, although many such models have been proposed over the years, they all bear a striking resemblance to Tuckman's original formulation. It is a true developmental model in the sense that, according to Tuckman, each stage must be completed before the group can move to the next. In the first stage, *forming,* team members assemble prior to beginning their work as a team, and nominally engage their task, while taking the measure of one another. In the second stage, *storming,* the team members argue, debate, posture, preen, and otherwise compete for status and social support; during this stage little work is actually accomplished. The third stage, *norming,* begins once the team members have established their informal pecking order and alliances. In the third stage the group decides on its operational procedures: who will do what and when, how to know if something has been done correctly, how to determine if a person is performing appropriately, and so on. The final stage, *performing,* concerns actually doing the work of the team. It is only after the group has finished storming and norming that it can truly begin functioning as a team.

The Tuckman model describes the process of team development. However, we need a prescriptive account of how a manager or a consultant should go about building a team. Here I draw on the work of Curphy (2004), whose model seems sensible and has a proven track record—it has been used with a number of public and private companies, including several very large, multinational firms, and it has been used with teams at all levels in those organizations. Curphy broke the elements of team building into seven components, which he labeled mission, talent, norms, buy-in, power, morale, and results. Each component is a kind of task the team must complete before it is ready to move on to the next component. Curphy used a team assessment process to create a profile across these seven components; indeed, creating such a profile is essential for further team development (all interventions at the individual or team level should be preceded by a competent assessment). The developmental components are as follows:

1. *Mission.* The mission component of team building involves setting a common direction for the team by clarifying the team's purpose and goals, setting performance standards, and aligning team members' goals with the team's goals. In some cases, the team builder may work with team members to sort out these issues; in other cases, the issues are decided by higher powers. However, Curphy argued, who makes the decisions is much less important than ensuring that everyone on the team understands what the team is trying to accomplish and what their role is in making the team successful. Teams that are clear about mission have much lower levels of role ambiguity and conflict. Mission is probably the most important component contributing to team performance because it drives all the other subsequent components. Mission defines the kind of talent needed on the team, the rules (norms) by which the team will operate, and the equipment and budget (power) needed. Every exercise in team building should begin by resolving the issues associated with mission.

2. *Talent.* A high-performing team will have the appropriate mix of talent. Curphy's model recommends evaluating the talent of current or potential members of a team using standardized assessments. There are three considerations for evaluating team members. First, are they good team players? The ability to perform as a team player can be determined using any well-validated inventory of normal per-

sonality such as the HPI (Hogan & Hogan, 1995). As noted earlier in this chapter, persons with above average scores for Adjustment, Interpersonal Sensitivity, and Prudence are good team players in principle. Second, consider the principle tasks of the team and classify them according to the Holland model. If the key tasks are realistic and conventional (in Holland's terms), then persons with above average scores for HPI Prudence and below average scores for HPI Sociability will perform best, and so on around the Holland hexagon (cf. Driskell, Hogan, & Salas, 1987). That is, as noted earlier, team tasks make distinctive demands on performance, and there is a personality style that is related to effective performance in each task. The third consideration when evaluating the talent of a team concerns the degree to which a team member's core values are consistent with culture of the team, as defined by the value profile for the team. As noted earlier, the values profile of individuals and teams can be assessed using the Motives, Values, Preferences Inventory (MVPI; Hogan & Hogan, 1996). We can summarize this section by noting that, to evaluate the talent of a team, the individual team members (present or potential) should be assessed to determine (a) their suitability to work as part of a team, (b) their fit with the primary team task, and (c) their fit with the team culture.

3. *Norms.* Once team members have been selected and clearly understand the team's goals and purposes, then the norm component of team development becomes important. Norms are the rules that regulate how teams make decisions, conduct meetings, hold members accountable, and share information. There are three points about norms that should be noted. First, the norms (regarding decision making, meetings, accountability, etc.) should be driven by the team's purposes and goals. Second, if the team is not explicit about defining its norms, other norms will simply evolve over time. However, these carelessly evolved norms may very well function in ways that are contrary to the proper operation of the team. When teams evolve unselfconsciously, they may evolve in self-defeating ways. Third, the universe of possible norms is extensive, but some norms are more important than others. Specifically, norms involving decision making, communication, meetings, and accountability are the most important for proper team performance. High-performing teams are very clear about how decisions get made. These teams also have rules about the confidentiality of team meetings, about when team members speak for themselves and when they speak for the

team, about how controversial topics should be raised in meetings, and about how team member accountability is defined. Teams become dysfunctional when they fail to establish explicit norms about decision making, communication, meeting performance, and accountability, or fail to ask themselves if the rules they have adopted are still needed and useful.

4. *Buy-in.* Just because team members understand a team's goals and operating rules does not mean they will necessarily be committed to them. It is not uncommon for team members to assent overtly to these matters, and then proceed as they please. In such cases, the team lacks buy-in. In teams with high levels of buy-in, the members believe in the team's goals and work hard to reach them. There are three ways to develop buy-in. The first is to develop a compelling team vision, overarching purpose, or raison d'etre. People in general want to be part of something bigger, nobler, and more important than themselves, and being part of a high-performing team can serve this purpose. The degree to which this is possible, however, significantly depends on the match between team members' personal values and the goals of the team. Some leaders are particularly skilled at being able to align team members' personal values with team goals. A second requirement for by-in concerns the credibility of the team leader. When team members question the leader's judgment and agenda, they will withhold their commitment. However, if they trust a leader's expertise and integrity, they usually find it easy to commit to the team's goals. Finally, if team members are involved in establishing the goals and norms of the team, their buy-in is facilitated, if not guaranteed.

5. *Power.* Power can be defined as the control of resources that are in high demand. Teams with power have the authority to make their own decisions, and they have the equipment, time, facilities, and funds needed to accomplish their goals. Conversely, teams with low power lack the discretion to make their own decisions and the resources to get things done. To increase the power of a team, team members must persuade senior people in the organization to give them more decision making latitude and additional resources, or they will need to redefine and scale back their goals in view of their mismatch with the power available. However, teams typically believe that they lack sufficient time, resources, and deci-

sion-making authority to achieve their goals; the reality is that they usually have enough of these resources to be successful. Good teams find ways to work effectively with what they have, or find ways to acquire additional resources. Dysfunctional teams are preoccupied with fretting about their perceived lack of support rather than finding ways to improvise and achieve their goals. They also tend to find or erect imaginary barriers to progress. Someone on the team must challenge the team's assumptions and break down the imaginary barriers if the team is to succeed.

6. *Morale.* Morale and cohesion concern the degree to which a team sticks together. All teams contain differences in values among team members, workload inequities, miscommunication, and implicit rivalries; these disjunctions combine, in every team, to create tension and interpersonal conflict. For a team to be effective, the members must devise ways to recognize and deal with conflict, and do so in a routine and equitable manner. When teams try to ignore interpersonal conflict either by denial or by telling team members to get over it, morale will begin to decline. When morale falls below a tipping point, a team will become dysfunctional, regardless of how well it has managed the earlier components of performance. It is also the case that resolving conflicts is an ongoing process rather than something that can be accomplished once and for all. One popular way of dealing with conflict is team-building programs such as outdoor learning or ropes courses. Typically, these interventions have little long-term impact on conflict because the conflict will often be a symptom of underlying issues such as poorly defined goals, roles, performance standards, or accountability norms. That is, conflict is often the result of not dealing adequately with prior issues in team development.

7. *Results.* The first six stages of the Curphy model concern how to build a team. The results component concerns what the team actually accomplishes. High-performing teams get good results because they have successfully attended to the first six stages. Ineffective teams can improve their performance by identifying and fixing problems in the first six components. The model is both descriptive and prescriptive. It describes the components involved in building an effective team, and it prescribes their use to enhance the performance of dysfunctional teams.

CONCLUSION

The literature on teams and groups has historically ignored two issues that I regard as essential. First, until perhaps 10 years ago, the team literature ignored the topic of effective team performance. In my view, effectiveness is the primary consideration when analyzing teams; it is the target at which every discussion should be aimed. Second, because the study of teams originated in sociology and social psychology, it has traditionally ignored the topic of personality. In my view, personality is the key to effective team performance. That team researchers have ignored performance is their problem; that they have ignored personality is to a substantial degree the fault of personality psychologists. The best known personality psychologists—Freud, Jung, Adler, Horney, Erikson, Allport, and Maslow—focus exclusively on intrapsychic dynamics, on interior lives, on personality from the inside. In contrast with this powerful intrapsychic tradition, I believe that (a) what happens on the inside reflects what has happened on the outside—our identities reflect our past interactions with family, friends, and colleagues; and (b) the most consequential part of our lives takes place in public, in interaction with family, friends, and colleagues, leaving us to reflect on those events in private. This emphasis on life in public points to the role of personality in team performance.

People are nested in teams, and teams are nested in organizations. People become part of teams by occupying roles. There are two powerful reasons why people need their roles. First, our identities, the core of our psychological beings, are created by playing roles in public; outside of our roles we have little to say to one another and as social beings, we need to have something to say. Thus we need our roles, which connect us to our teams, groups, families, or communities, for our psychological survival. Second, we need to be part of a team, group, family, or community for our physical survival. Isolated primates, including humans, do not live very long.

Personality must be defined in two ways: (a) in terms of interpersonal style; and (b) in terms of identity. Personality influences team performance in three ways. First, certain interpersonal styles equip certain people to be good team players, and the evidence is quite clear that bad team players disrupt team performance. Second, certain interpersonal styles equip people to play certain occupational roles better than others. For example, persons who are extroverted and impulsive make poor long-distance truck drivers or air traffic controllers, but good sales personnel—and the data are quite clear on this. Third, personal identity is defined by a person's core values. Every team or group has a culture defined by the shared values of its members. People perform best on teams where their values are congruent with the values of the team, and the data are quite clear on this.

In this chapter I have deliberately minimized any discussion of leadership. However, as chapter 3 indicates, personality strongly influences leadership performance, and leadership performance strongly influences team performance. Obviously, then, personality also affects team performance through the role of team leader.

5

The Secret Life of Organizations: Personality and Organizational Theory

In chapter 4, I argued that (a) teams are composed of individuals, (b) team phenomena are distinct from individual phenomena, but (c) team phenomena can nonetheless be reduced to principles of personality psychology. In this chapter I argue that (a) teams are nested in organizations, (b) team and organizational phenomena are different, but (c) organizational phenomena can also be reduced to principles of personality psychology.

Concerning the claim that organizational phenomena can be understood in terms of individual psychology, consider how consultants who work with organizations to enhance their effectiveness gather and use data. They base their recommendations about organizational changes on survey data; that is, they ask incumbents to comment on their experience in an organization. They ask incumbents about such things as their level of commitment, motivation, satisfaction with compensation, feelings of empowerment, ability to make decisions, access to information, feelings of role clarity, and confidence in senior management. Based on summaries of these individual perceptions, consultants diagnose organizational functioning and formulate strategies for improvement. They use personality data—individual perceptions—to build models of organizational functioning. In their actual behavior, many organizational consultants endorse the major thesis of this chapter.

The following anecdote illustrates the ways in which team and organizational processes are different. We know a young man who is a medical specialist in the Army National Guard; because of his unique skills, he could expect preferred treatment. He believed his National Guard unit would be sent to Iraq in 2005. Although eligible for a special deferment, he reported that he intended to go to Iraq with his fellow Guardsmen because "they were a team." This is a common story. Survey research with the U.S. Army after World War II indicated that the reason many soldiers fought had nothing to do with their allegiance to the country or its principles, to the military, or to the stated goals of the war. Rather, they fought out of a sense of loyalty to their immediate comrades in arms. There is often a kind of accountability and cohesion among team members that does not exist between people and the organizations where they work.

This chapter concerns the links between individual personality and organizational processes. The overall argument is that certain processes operate in every organization; these processes will unfold regardless of the people who are in charge of, or working in, the organization; and that these processes reflect the dynamics of individual personality. Moreover, these processes seem to operate outside the awareness of individual incumbents; they form the organizational unconscious. I refer to these processes as the secret life of organizations.

In a nutshell, this chapter outlines a personality-based theory of organizations. Many psychologists are uninterested in organizational theory. For example, most discussions of organizational development ignore organizational theory (cf. Austin & Bartunek, 2003; Warclawski & Church, 2002). This amounts to trying to fix a car without understanding the principles underlying its construction.

Much organizational theory reflects the perspective of structural sociology (cf. Selznick, 1957). From Durkheim to the present, sociologists argue that societies create the organizations that they need, that structural factors in organizations (e.g., climate and culture) govern the behavior of the incumbents, and these factors are largely independent of the wishes and desires of individuals. Sociologists typically resist efforts to reduce organizational phenomena to underlying principles of human behavior. In contrast, this chapter is firmly reductionistic; it argues that most organizational phenomena reflect the desires, actions, and choices of specific individuals—usually the people in positions of power.

WHAT IS AN ORGANIZATION?

Organizations can be defined as "resource pools" (Buchanan, 1977). In this view, organizations come into existence when individuals place their resources (money, skill, contacts) under some form of central control so that they can be used collectively for the benefit of the individuals who created the organizations. Organizations must then establish some rules for the use and distribution of their resources. The sum of these formal rules is the organizational structure, and it defines how the collective resources should be used to reach organizational goals. Although the structure determines the behavior of incumbents, the structure does not cause the behavior. The behavior is caused by individual efforts to get along and get ahead.

People have been writing books about organizations for a surprisingly long time. The Egyptian Ptah-hotep wrote the first known guide on how to manage an organization, on papyrus, in 2700 BC. Several books on management were written by business people following the Industrial Revolution that exploded in the mid-19th century. Taylor's (1911) guide to scientific management, which used experimental methods to find solutions to everyday business problems, was the first important empirical work on the subject, and many of Taylor's prescriptions are still valid today; for example, people should be assigned to jobs based on the match between a job's demands and a person's capabilities.

MAX WEBER AND ORGANIZATIONAL THEORY

Weber (1947), the brilliant and deeply troubled German social theorist, provided one of the first (and in many ways the most influential) discussions of organizational theory. It is worth noting that Weber's ideas are completely consistent with a personality-based theory of organizations—probably because Weber read Freud (e.g., Freud's and Weber's ideas about charismatic leadership are quite similar).

Weber described three ideal types of organizations: the traditional, the revolutionary, and the bureaucratic. These are often seen as forming a kind of developmental hierarchy, with traditional organizations coming first, followed by a revolution, followed by a bureaucracy. In this view, traditional organizations (the Medieval Catholic Church) are eventually overthrown by charismatic revolutionary leaders (Martin Luther); the revolutionaries establish a reformed organization. After a while, the process of "the routinization of charisma" sets in, and the new organiza-

tional structures become increasingly formal and rigid. Weber is normally interpreted as saying that revolutionary organizations inevitably
turn into bureaucracies, and bureaucracies are an ideal end state—according to Weber, bureaucracies are the only rational way to structure
an organization because they are based on rules, accountability, and
transparency.

I think the foregoing is probably a misreading of Weber; for sure it is a
misreading of history. A better historical reading is as follows. Most human societies (with the exception of hunter-gatherer groups), from the
beginning of agriculture (13,000 years ago) to the present, have been
autocracies, which are inevitably overcome by revolutions, and which
then give way to subsequent autocracies (cf. Diamond, 1997). Consider
the events that unfolded in the small West African country of Togo in
2005. Togo was part of a wave of African countries that gained independence from their colonial masters in the 1960s. The first "elected" president of Togo, Sylvanus Olympia, was killed in 1963 in a military coup
d'etat. The man who shot him, Eyadema Gnassingbe, staged his own
coup in 1967 and ruled for 37 years with the support of a succession of
French governments. Although not a butcher or kleptomaniac, he ruled
with an iron hand and ruined his country's economy. He died in February 2005; Togo's military leaders promptly appointed Eyadema's son,
Faure Gnassingbe, as president, in violation of the country's constitution. Faure and the army leaders rewrote the constitution to legitimize
his presidency, much to the consternation of the populace, who hoped
to see a transition into a modern, rational, democratic government—a
Weberian bureaucracy. This is a typical story: One traditional society is
replaced by another after a revolution, but the new government
behaves much like the one it replaced.

Governments by warlords who gain power through force of arms seem
to be the default setting for human societies. Philip of Macedonia, Julius
Caesar, Genghis Khan, Charlemagne, Henry the VIII of England, Gamal
Attaturk, Josef Stalin, Mao Tse Tung, and Saddam Hussein were all warlords; they established social orders that provided incumbents with predictability and protection from outside invaders, and they did so in return
for taxes and tributes. These traditional societies are characterized by ex-
ploitation, status based on politics and personal preferences, arbitrary
laws, and economic stagnation, and they are the most traditional and
common form of human social organization over the past 13,000 years.

But there are always pretenders to the warlord's throne. From time to
time, charismatic figures emerge who are able to attract a following and

mount a challenge to the established order. When Napoleon Bonaparte, Adolph Hitler, or Fidel Castro succeeded, a new revolutionary order was established. This is Weber's second organizational type. After the revolution, there will be a period of foment and "progress," but in reality one warlord has replaced another. From the perspective of the ordinary citizen, not much will change. History consists of one autocratic ruling group giving way to another, unless something radical happens.

Weber thought there was an alternative to the seemingly endless cycle of autocratic administration and revolutionary replacement. From a scientific perspective, there is a right way and many wrong ways to do anything. Adam Smith argued that, if a country's economy were rationally administered, the welfare of every member of society would inevitably improve. In the tradition of Smith, Weber proposed that bureaucracies are the only rational alternative to the traditional hierarchies of warlords and their revolutionary successors. In a bureaucracy, the governing principle is the progressive betterment of all the incumbents, not the personal enrichment of the people at the top. People are assigned to positions of authority based on their talent and qualifications, and then paid and promoted based on their performance—as opposed to their personal relationships. Decisions are based on impersonal rules designed to maximize the performance of the organization. People comply with the rules of the bureaucracy because doing so is the path to better pay and promotions. The established rules and procedures of a bureaucracy promote the welfare of the entire organization precisely because they control the self-seeking tendencies of the aspiring warlords within the organization. A rational bureaucracy is the only governmental form in which a capitalist economy can flourish. The two alternative forms of government (traditional and revolutionary) pursue ruinous economic policies, designed to benefit the ruling elites. A rational bureaucracy is an ideal, something to be striven for, rather than an inexorable historical development. This is a better reading of Weber, and the starting point for the rest of this chapter.

TEN INEVITABLE THEMES

The primary claim of this chapter is that certain themes can be found in every organization. These themes inevitably recur because they are rooted in human nature, and they are often (perhaps usually) unnoticed. As noted earlier, they are part of the secret lives of organizations, they are part of the organizational unconscious. The following discussion describes 10 of these themes.

Organizations as Pyramid Schemes

The first theme concerns the fact that, in every organization, resources flow upward in an increasing volume and those at the top usually benefit greatly. In Dakar, Senegal, the streets are full of scrawny, undernourished boys chanting religious verses and begging from the passers by. They are the *talibes,* or beggar boys, of Senegal; they are sent out into the streets each day by religious leaders called *marabouts,* and they are expected to beg. Each boy has a daily quota ranging from 250 to 650 francs ($0.50–$1.30), plus whatever else they can persuade people to drop in their tin cans: sugar cubes, biscuits, milk powder, kola nuts. If they fail to meet their quotas, they are often beaten by the *marabouts,* who live on the earnings of the beggar boys.

This reveals an underlying reality of virtually every organization; almost all organizations are forms of a pyramid scheme. Charles Ponzi (1882–1949), an Italian speculator, gave us the eponymous Ponzi scheme: People are recruited into organizations and then make payments to others above them in the hierarchy. They, in turn, expect to be paid by newer recruits below them in the hierarchy. In the medieval Catholic Church, parishioners paid the priests for assistance with the divinity, the priests paid the bishops, and the bishops paid the cardinals, who paid the Pope. Senior officers in the military enjoy perquisites that the lower ranks can only dream about. This fact is denoted by the phrase rank has its privileges (RHIP); this fact is justified by the phrase rank has its responsibilities (RHIR). The salary differentials between CEOs of U.S. companies and their workers are as enormous as they are ridiculous. As an assistant professor with good academic credentials, poor pay, and working 80 hours a week, I was invited to the lavish, university-sponsored home of the president, a retired politician. The contrast in the lifestyles of an assistant professor and the president caused me to begin questioning how equitably resources are distributed in all organizations.

How are these pyramid schemes able to persist without being overthrown by those at the bottom of the hierarchy? Four factors explain the persistence of the power relations in organizations. First, like the participants in a Ponzi scheme, many people at the bottom believe that, if they work hard and support the organization, they may be able to rise to the top and enjoy the benefits that accrue to such status.

Second, the founders and subsequent generations of leaders create reasonably complex stories, theories, myths, and explanations about why their organization is structured as it is. These are the urban legends that people accept as true because they make sense out of daily activities; they assign meaning to current practices; and all people have strong, innate needs for meaning, purpose, and structure in their lives. The most potent and complex of these overarching justifications are, of course, religious; Marx was at least partially correct when he noted that religion is the "opiate of the people," whereby the "bourgeoisie keep the proletariat in chains." There are always myths regarding why a society or an organization is structured as it is, and people allow themselves to believe in the myths.

Third, people need to be part of a group to survive. All the important human needs (companionship, sustenance, status, and meaning) are met primarily by participating in group processes; there are important benefits that accrue to organizational membership, resulting in a kind of quid pro quo. If one wants to be part of the group, one must show loyalty to the group—"You need to go along to get along," as former U.S. President Lyndon Johnson used to say. Conversely, if one criticizes the existing social system, if one violates the rules and procedures too overtly, one will be sanctioned. If one ignores the sanctions, they will escalate. If one continues to criticize the governance structure and ignore the rules, one will be invited to leave the group. If one refuses to leave voluntarily, force will be applied. One of the fictions of every society is that people's compliance with society's rules and procedures is voluntary; the reality is that the ultimate source of individual compliance is the threat, and occasional administration, of violence. The threat of violence encourages the acceptance of the status quo.

The final reason that people accept and support social organizations that primarily serve the interests of the people at the top derives from a fundamental principle of personality psychology. Bourdieu (1984) called it misrecognition; Marx called it false consciousness, Sartre (1960) called it self-deception or double-mindedness, and Freud called it repression, but they were referring to the same phenomenon. When people are confronted with facts, data, or evidence that challenge important beliefs (e.g., there is a Santa Claus; our president cares about the welfare of all citizens), people pretend not to notice the evidence, and then pretend not to notice that they are not noticing (MacIntyre, 1958). By ignoring the evidence, they are able to maintain their comforting illusions. In this way, organizations survive, persist, and even prosper—based on individual psychological dynamics.

Who Shall Rule?

According to the political scientists, the fundamental question in human affairs is this: Who shall rule? This suggests that the principal dynamic in every organization is the individual search for power. Like all human characteristics, striving for power is an individual differences variable. Thus, a small number of people in each organization will compete furiously for power, most people will just do their jobs and watch the power plays unfold, and a small number of people are usually oblivious to the meaning of the events unfolding around them. Most of the significant activity and most of the new initiatives in any organization come from those players who want to advance themselves.

Psychologists by and large either ignore or minimize the human drive for power; however, writers from other disciplines understand its importance. Consider, for example, Bertrand Russell. Along with Alfred North Whitehead, Russell wrote *Principia Mathematica,* which analyzes the logical foundations of modern mathematics. He received the Nobel Prize for Literature in 1950, and his acceptance speech is pertinent to this discussion. He began by observing that "most discussions of politics and political theory take insufficient account of psychology ... . If politics is to become scientific ... it is imperative that our political thinking should penetrate more deeply into the springs of human action." By the springs of human action, Russell meant, of course, human motivation, the core of personality (Frenz, 1969).

Russell noted that the most important human desires are important precisely because they have political consequences; that is, they drive politicians. He focused on four of these, which he listed in order of increasing importance. The first is acquisitiveness (security), a desire to acquire the resources necessary for one's survival. Acquisitiveness is "the mainspring of the capitalist system," and good capitalists can never have enough money and resources. The second desire is rivalry (competition for status), which is triggered by jealousy. So powerful is rivalry that many men will "cheerfully face impoverishment if they can thereby secure complete ruin for their rivals." The third desire is vanity or glory (recognition). The need for glory is insatiable—the more we are talked about, the more we want to be talked about—and vanity is so attractive that humans have attributed the same desire to their deity, "whom they imagine avid for continual praise" (Frenz, 1969).

The fourth and most important desire is power; power "is by far the strongest motive in the lives of important men." People exercise power by making others do things they would rather not do; consequently, "the man who is actuated by the love of power is more apt to inflict pain than to permit pleasure." Russell notes finally that "It is this sort of thing which makes the love of power such a dangerous motive" (cf. Frenz, 1969).

Weber noted that, in even the most professional, disciplined, impersonal, and formal bureaucracies, the people at the top often behave like oriental despots. In addition, they face perpetual battles with their ambitious subordinates who also seek power, and they spend most of their time managing the power struggles of their subordinates. After Weber, the French sociologist Bourdieu is the great modern student of power in organizations (cf. Swartz, 1997). Bourdieu argued that the struggle for power and control and the desire to outperform one's peers along a dimension of status is the fundamental theme underlying organizational life. Thus, every organization is a cockpit of competition that provides a context for the individual pursuit of distinction. Bourdieu also noted that the incumbents of organizations persistently ignore this underlying reality of organizational life.

Somewhat closer to home, Cyert and Marsh (1963) argued that competition for, and control over, resources (power) is the goal of every principal actor in an organization. Consequently, the structures of organizations are developed by powerful people to grant or deny certain other people access to the resources. Similarly, Hambrick (1994), in his study of top management groups, argued that top group members are primarily concerned with status, with becoming the group leader or CEO. These individuals "who almost by definition tend to be aggressive, hierarchy-minded achievers" (p. 179) are preoccupied with power and are engaged in a "succession tournament." Again, the principal dynamic in every organization is the individual search for power.

These observations lead to three additional conclusions. First, power transitions are defining moments in every organization. For example, the majority of the businesses in the world are family-controlled, from unsung millions of modest firms to commercial giants such as Wal-Mart, Samsung or Hyundai. Problems occur when the children do not want to work in the family business after the parents are gone. This typically sets off a fight concerning who next shall rule.

Second, the way to get something done in an organization is to provide power seekers with a vehicle for advancement. I have consulted with organizations for over 30 years; in my experience, clients typically do not ask for help because it will make their organizations function better. They engage consultants because they think that the consultants' "programs" will make them look good. In a real sense, clients adopt management interventions for perfectly rational reasons—career advancement. This also explains why, when the clients receive their promotions, the consulting relationship often ends; the reason is that the new people want to find ways to differentiate themselves by introducing a new consulting intervention.

Third, the ubiquitous struggle for power explains why there is so much resistance to change in organizations. Change holds out the possibility that power relations will change. Those who expect to gain power will endorse change, whereas those who anticipate losing power will resist change. In late 2004, there was considerable discussion regarding the need to reorganize the U.S. CIA to make information flow more efficiently. As the *New York Times* noted repeatedly, the entrenched senior administrators at the CIA were more interested in preserving their power than in promoting national defense, and worked quietly but persistently to resist reorganization.

Three Kinds of Power

People find the loss of power profoundly stressful and history is replete with examples of the lengths to which people will go to gain or retain power. It is important, therefore, to specify the sources of individual power. Power is best defined in terms of the control of resources, particularly resources that others covet or need; these resources can be money, access to information, or force (Pfeffer, 1992). In every organization, there are three sources of power. First, there is inherited power: Owners, founders, their chosen favorites, and other entitled people have power because they started the organization, or because they have been there the longest, and they have the means necessary to maintain their authority. Second, there is power based on personal charisma and positive relations with others; some people can have their way because subordinates and peers like or respect them (French & Raven, 1959). Third, there is power based on position and the legitimate rules of the organization. Some people can have their way because of the formal position they occupy (March & Olsen, 1982). All three forms of power are somewhat transitory and can disappear overnight.

The Tension Between Individual and Organizational Goals

There is a constant tension in every organization between the rules and procedures designed to maximize the effectiveness and success of an organization and the proclivities of individual actors who want to use the organizational resources for self-advancement. Human nature is such that, unless a rational governing structure is imposed on an organization and then vigorously maintained, people will begin working for themselves and not the organization. Moreover, even though a rational governing structure has been established, a few individuals will nonetheless begin trying to subvert it. In Benjamin Franklin's last speech before the U.S. Congress, he argued that the American experiment with constitutional democracy would inevitably fail because selfish politicians would sooner or later find ways to manipulate the system for their own purposes, to the detriment of society as a whole.

The Origins of Rules

As Weber noted, organizations become steadily more rule bound over time. His generalization is correct, but the interesting question concerns why this is so. Weber argued that the rules were needed to make the organization more efficient, but there is an alternative account for the accumulation of rules. Imagine a new organization, full of fire, inspiration, and innovative tendencies. Inevitably someone will begin to cheat the system by claiming unauthorized vacation time or travel expenses, or by conducting personal business on company time. When the cheating is discovered, rules will be put in place to control that particular form of misconduct. Then someone will find another way to cheat the company, and more rules will be established. Rules will be implemented one at a time to curb each particular form of organizational misconduct, and the rules will steadily accumulate.

The law of nomological nonbiodegradability (Hogan & Henley, 1969) predicts that rules, once in place, rarely go away. This means that, as organizations grow, their rule structures thicken. Mature organizations have so many rules that most innovations will require breaking a rule, unless provisions are made for this. Successful innovators within an organization need to break rules, and doing so provides ammunition for their critics and rivals. It also tends to bring innovation to an end. The larger point is that the inevitable process of rule accumulation in organizations is more a function of efforts to control miscreants than efforts to improve efficiency.

The Paradox of Power

There is an interesting anomaly associated with the pursuit of power. The higher one rises in a bureaucratic organization (regardless of whether it is private enterprise or government), the harder it is to get one's way. A funny anecdote from the administration of former U.S. President Jimmy Carter exemplifies the point. It seems that a mouse died inside the wall in the Oval Office. It began to stink, and President Carter, despite strenuous efforts, was unable to have it removed.

Warlords have direct relationships with their subordinates, whom they have personally chosen. In addition, the rules regarding how warlords treat their subordinates are usually flexible. If a warlord gives an order and it is not obeyed, direct sanctions may be swiftly applied. In a bureaucracy, however, a person's relationships with his or her subordinates are formal. Many of these subordinates were in the organization before the CEO or manager in question arrived, and will be there after the person leaves. It is usually rather difficult to punish incompetence or insubordination in large organizations, and then only after formal review processes have been followed. In addition, passive aggressive behavior on the part of subordinates is extremely difficult to detect or sanction when it is detected. Passive aggressive personalities are skilled at defying authority (e.g.,"When did you need that report? I'm sorry, the computers are down, and it won't be ready in time.").

Senior managers in big organizations have a lot of power, defined in terms of access to information, personal contacts with powerful others, and budgets, but they have a limited ability to make specific individuals do things they do not want to do. In addition, to implement any new initiative takes a lot of concentrated time and energy. Senior managers are beset by new problems, almost by the minute. Many of these problems are political and come from the machinations of their rivals and immediate subordinates. So, regardless of the amount of power they have at their disposal, they do not have extended blocks of time to focus on specific change initiatives and drive them to completion in the way they envision. This, then, accounts for the paradox of power.

Leadership and Top Management Groups

Common sense suggests that leadership is an important determinant of the fate of organizations, but many writers challenge this assumption. For example, from a sociological perspective, organizational success depends primarily on demographic, economic, and historical forces that are beyond the control of any individual. Not surprisingly, organizational researchers with a sociological orientation have consistently disputed the view that leadership affects organizational performance in any significant way (cf. Salancik & Pfeffer, 1977). World wars and widespread economic downturns can obviously swamp the best laid strategies of any leader, but the logic of this book dictates that leadership must be an important determinant of the fate of organizations.

Beginning with papers by Day and Lord (1988) and Thomas (1988), data have steadily accumulated demonstrating the financial impact that leaders have on their organizations. For example, Barrick, Day, Lord, and Alexander (1991) showed that, compared to average performing executives, high performers add an additional $25 million in value to their organizations during their tenure. Similarly, Joyce, Nohria, and Roberson (2003) reported that CEOs account for about 14% of the variance in the financial performance of their organizations. The data show quite clearly that leadership is a determinant of organizational success.

The next question concerns the mechanisms by which leaders impact the functioning of their organizations. The answer is they exercise influence through their immediate subordinates, whose influence (for good or ill) then radiates through the system. In an important paper, Harter, Schmidt, and Hayes (2002) showed that the personalities of managers directly influence the satisfaction of their subordinates, and that the satisfaction level of the subordinates directly influences the performance of the organization. In a meta-analysis using 198,514 employees in 7,939 business units, they reported correlations near .40, at the business-unit level, between employee satisfaction and turnover, customer loyalty, and financial performance. So the personalities of managers affect employee satisfaction, which then affects business unit performance.

The small but important literature on top management groups (Hambrick, 1994) further demonstrates how the personalities of leaders affect the performance of organizations, and the effect is real but indirect. The general model is that leader personality influences the dynamics and culture of the top management group, and the characteristics of the top management group influence the performance of the organization. In a very interesting paper, Peterson, Smith, Martorana, and Owens (2003), using data from CEOs of 17 very large corporations (e.g., IBM, Coca-Cola, Disney, Xerox, CBS, Chrysler, General Motors), reported correlations in the .50 range between CEO personality and various aspects of the functioning of the top management group (e.g., cohesiveness, corruption, risk tolerance). Then they showed that the characteristics of the top management group (cohesiveness, etc.) are substantially correlated with such business outcomes as income, sales growth, return on investment, and return on assets.

What are the personality-based lessons in this? There are three. First, the influence of leadership (for good or for ill) is silent and inexorable. Specifically, leadership influences long-term organizational outcomes through the cumulative consequences of individual decisions, and decisions reflect personality. There are decisions to go forward that turn out badly (Time Warner's merger with AOL), and there are decisions not to go forward that turn out badly (Xerox's decision not to go into the manufacturing of personal computers). In the 1970s, a small group of leaders at the American Psychological Association (APA) decided to buy *Psychology Today,* a commercial magazine devoted to popularizing psychology. Although the magazine was failing under professional management, its problems rapidly increased when a group of academics began to manage it. The subsequent failure of the magazine put the APA into bankruptcy, but as is so often the case, those who made the ruinously bad decision were never held accountable.

Second, as Weber (and Hambrick, 1994) pointed out, the members of the top management group are engaged in an intense struggle for power that, for the most part, people pretend does not exist. These contenders for power create fiefdoms, spheres of personal influence and control that they use to advance their interests, often at the expense of the larger organization. In addition, according to Hambrick (1994), over time top management teams can become dysfunctional as success begets complacency and then possible failure:

> These are well known trajectories documented in prior research … . Highly interactive, collaborative top management groups in one context become loose constellations of executive talent in another context … . A top management group with low integration has difficulty (1) achieving a shared awareness … of new environmental imperatives, (2) formulating concerted responses … to those imperatives, and (3) implementing plans. Accustomed to independence, separateness, "running their own shows," these groups … cannot get their act together. (p. 200)

The point is that leadership impacts organizational performance through top management teams, which can become dysfunctional over time.

Third, although the importance of leadership for the fate of organizations is well documented, the people who are responsible for choosing new CEOs rarely choose them based on their leadership skills. Rather, they choose new CEOs for a variety of personal and idiosyncratic reasons. Carlton Fiorina was Vice President for Marketing at Lucent, where her leadership style was characterized as arrogant, insensitive, and self-dramatizing, and where her staff was eager for her to leave. When Hewlett-Packard (HP) began searching for a new CEO in 1999, one very powerful board member wanted HP to merge with Compaq, another computer manufacturer. He lobbied the rest of the board to hire Fiorina, not because of her talent for leadership, but because she was willing to pursue the merger that he wanted. At HP her leadership style was characterized by arrogance and a penchant for self-dramatization. The merger turned out badly and Fiorina was fired.

The Origins of Psychological Taxation

In a pride of lions, there will be two groups. One group will hunt game and protect the pride's territory, at considerable personal risk. A second and much smaller group will be "free riders"; they do not hunt and they do not protect the territory; they live off the efforts of the others. So it seems to go with group-living animals.

Every large organization has two groups of people. The first and usually largest group contains people who perform key work, the activities that actually define the organization. For a railroad, these are the people who operate and maintain the trains and switching yards; for a university, these are the people who do the teaching and research. The second and much smaller group contains people who control important parts of the organization without contributing to its core work. These are the politicians who reside in the executive suite. Many of them are free riders—they participate in the profits of an organization without contributing in a direct way to the major work.

I talked with the brilliant and hard-working manager of a branch office of a very large financial services firm. This woman had built an enormously successful practice despite the sexism and lack of support from the senior executives in the organization, whose activities are frequently reported on in the *New York Times*. The CEO, a cold, aloof tyrant widely hated for his leadership, had recently hired a man with good "people skills" to put a friendly face on the organization. The branch manager had met this person, along with most of the other senior executives. She remarked that, "In all candor, I am not very impressed with those people; they are good politicians, but they are not especially bright, and none of them has ever built a business."

There are many free riders in larger society, including people at all levels of government. The October 17, 2005, issue of *The New Republic* contained profiles of 15 senior officials in the U.S. government who were hired based on personal contacts, who were unqualified for their jobs, who were widely disliked by their staffs, and whose performance was dreadful. The emergence of free riders is inevitable and inexorable, and they constitute a kind of psychological taxation; supporting them is a cost that productive people have to bear. Each organization has only a limited carrying capacity, so when the number of free riders—compared to the number of actual contributors—passes a certain point, something like the French Revolution or a mass defection of talent becomes hard to avoid.

The Origins of Organizational Culture

Schneider (1987) noted that organizations become increasingly homogenous over time—that is, they develop a culture—and they do so in ways that are outside individual awareness. He began his analysis with Holland's (1997) view that the psychological environment of organizations (i.e., the culture) reflects the personalities of the dominant people in it. This is an important and clarifying insight—Holland defined environments in terms of the personal characteristics of the high-status people in them, and not by office locations, industry sectors, or organizational charts, which can be more easily measured. A paper by Miller, Kets de Vries, and Toulouse (1982) provides empirical support for Holland's generalization. Miller et al. (1982) noted that the behavior "in and around organizations [is] a function of the personalities and capacities of specific individuals" (p. 237). They then reviewed evidence showing that individual differences in CEOs' scores on locus of control (a generic measure of self-confidence) predicted the degree of innovation, risk taking, proactiveness, future orientation, dynamism, and heterogeneity of the environment, and environmental scanning in the organization.

Schneider described the origins of organizational culture in terms of five generalizations. First, as noted earlier, CEO personality influences or creates organizational culture. Second, the longer a CEO's tenure, the more he or she will shape and define the culture. Third, people whose personalities fit with an organization's culture will be attracted to that organization. Fourth, persons whose personalities are inconsistent with an organization's culture will tend to leave. Fifth, as a consequence of the foregoing, organizations become progressively more homogenous over time as defined by the personality characteristics of the incumbents. These five generalizations form the basis for Schneider's well-known attraction, selection, attrition (ASA) model. The ASA model is an important and well-documented generalization about how personality affects organizations in a silent but inexorable manner.

Schneider's analysis leads to two practical consequences. On the one hand, the fact that organizations become more homogenous over time is a dangerous outcome—homogenous organizations become one-dimensional and unable to respond to change. On the other hand, when hiring new CEOs and other senior management, organizations should take care to align the characteristics of their CEOs with the existing culture and business strategy, but they rarely do. An example occurred in 2005 when Hewlett-Packard, an old-line Silicon Valley engineering firm whose culture famously featured teamwork and quality, hired the flamboyant and marketing-oriented Carlton Fiorina as the new CEO; this mismatch led to stalled performance and Fiorina's subsequent departure.

The Garbage Can Model

The Hawthorne Experiments (Roethlisberger & Dickson, 1939) can be interpreted as showing that although employees typically follow organizational directives, they are also social beings with their own private motives. In contrast with classical economic models, which view organizations as unified actors pursuing rational choices, the Hawthorne studies suggest that people in organizations have their own agendas and will pursue them when they can, regardless of the consequences to the organizations. Moreover, rationality in organizations is "bounded" (March & Simon, 1958). The term *bounded rationality* refers to the fact that senior people in organizations never have enough information to make fully rational choices, whatever their intentions might be. This leads to the view that the decision-making processes in organizations are often "garbage cans" (March & Olsen, 1976).

The garbage can model refers to decision making in organizations with ambiguous goals, where the managers are constantly moving up or moving on, and where the managers have personal agendas and bounded rationality. Aspiring managers will identify problems, promote their possible solutions, and then move on; although the managers are gone, the problems and solutions that they have identified set an agenda that influences the future path of the organization, regardless of its connection to the past or the present. The point is that crucial organizational decisions are made by actors who are trying to advance their own careers, who are using incomplete information, and who are rarely in the organization long enough to see, or be held accountable for, the results of their decisions. This is one more way in which personality shapes the fate of organizations.

ORGANIZATIONAL EFFECTIVENESS

People always live in groups. Their welfare will depend on the success of the groups in which they live. For 99.9% of human history people lived in the groups where they were born. The modern world increasingly provides people with choices about the groups in which they live. Regardless of how much choice people have about where they live and work, their well-being will still depend on the success of the larger groups with which they align themselves. This fact points out the importance of understanding organizational effectiveness.

Despite the importance of the topic of organizational effectiveness, psychologists tend to avoid dealing with it. The managerial literature has taken the problem more seriously. Management theorists have used four general classes of variables to define effectiveness across a wide range of business organizations, and they are productivity, finances, customer service, and human resources.

Measures of productivity reflect efficiency in transforming inputs (capital, people, materials) into outputs (goods and services). Social psychologists (e.g., Katz & Kahn, 1978) also use this measure of organizational effectiveness. Indicators here include quantity and quality of products, sales per employee, and rate of innovation. Note that these measures compare an organization to itself; these measures overlook the fact that organizations are in competition with one another. It would be more appropriate, it seems, to norm these variables against industry averages.

The second category of effectiveness measures concerns financial indicators, two of which—market-based and accounting-based (Hirschey & Wichern, 1984)—are particularly important. Market-based measures represent perceptions of current and potential wealth creation. They reflect profitability and value to shareholders and are represented by total shareholder return, price-to-earnings ratio, and Tobin's Q ratio (market value divided by cost to replace assets). There is general agreement that market-based measures are superior to accounting data because they are less subject to manipulation (Anderson & Terrell, 2004). Nonetheless, accounting data do provide additional information relevant to organizational effectiveness (Hirschey & Wichern, 1984). Common examples include earnings per share, return on investment or assets or equity, earnings growth rates, and economic value added (operating profit less taxes and the cost of capital; Stern, Shiely, & Ross, 2001).

Customer service indexes are the third category of effectiveness measures; they concern customer satisfaction, retention, and growth. Market share is a common example of such a measure. The final category, human-resource-based measures, reflects how well an organization manages talent. Indexes in this group include rate of turnover, accident rates, and morale. Bench strength—the number and quality of future leaders—probably belongs here as well. An important point about customer and human-resource-based measures of effectiveness is that, although they are not reflected directly in the bottom line, they are crucial to sustaining productivity and financial performance. That is, if an organization achieves financial results while alienating customers and demoralizing employees, the organization will inevitably suffer. Taken together, these measures of business results map the domain of organizational effectiveness.

Ultimately, organizational effectiveness seems to depend on five factors or sets of considerations, all of which relate back to individual personalities. The first factor that determines the effectiveness of an organization is the talent of the workforce. More talented people will outperform less talented people, other things being equal. The talent level of a workforce is a direct function of the quality of the selection and evaluation procedures that management has chosen.

The second factor that determines the effectiveness of an organization is the motivation level of the workforce. A highly motivated but not overly talented group will outperform a talented but demoralized group. The motivation of the workforce is a direct function of the quality of the managers for whom they must work. Bad managers can (and do) demoralize any workforce.

The third factor that determines the effectiveness of an organization is the leadership skills of the management group. Putting an effective management group in place depends on the adequacy of the management selection and evaluation process, and that, ultimately, depends on the degree to which senior management cares about the issue.

The fourth factor determining the effectiveness of organizations is the business strategy. Deriving a rational business strategy requires doing research. CEOs are not researchers—if they were, they would not be CEOs. CEOs are, in Holland's (1997) terms, enterprising/conventional types (extroverted, ambitious, power seeking, and motivated by money); researchers are, in Holland's terms, investigative/artistic types (introverted, creative, and motivated by ideas). So CEOs often choose strategies that maximize individual agendas, allow incumbents to retain power, and otherwise make sense.

In any case, a competent strategy must consider the following issues: (a) a business model, (b) the competition, (c) sales and marketing, (d) execution and distribution, and (e) customer service. Any organization must determine what business it is in and how it will sustain itself financially. Then the organization must determine how it will position itself vis-à-vis its competition. These two issues are the core of most strategic planning efforts, but they are insufficient in themselves to make an organization effective. Next it must find ways to market and sell its unique product or offering. Having attracted customers, the organization must devise ways to get its products or offerings to its customers. Finally, the organization must be prepared to deal with issues of implementation and customer grievances. These issues are not psychological, they are strategic, formal, and structural, but people will be needed to do the sales, implementation and execution, and customer follow-up.

The final factor determining organizational effectiveness is having monitoring systems in place to evaluate, periodically, the talent level of the workforce, the motivational state of the workforce, the talent of the management team, and the effectiveness of the business strategy. It is the responsibility of the senior leadership in an organization to put these five components in place. Ultimately, then, good leadership is the key to organizational effectiveness.

It is pointless to inquire about the effectiveness of monopolies—the U.S. Coast Guard or the FBI—because they have no competition, but we can ask about the effectiveness of business organizations. The first question that comes up concerns the base rate of organizational effectiveness for modern businesses. I know of no research on this topic, but some data are always better than no data. An article using individual organizations as a unit of analysis, reports that 31% of the organizations they studied were "healthy," 53% were "unhealthy," and 15% could not be classified. The conclusion is that most organizations are ineffective, and this is because most organizations make hiring mistakes, most organizations have a large percentage of incompetent managers, most organizations do a poor job of strategic planning to compete effectively, and most organizations are lax in the process of self-monitoring and evaluation.

Most organizations make mistakes in the way they handle all five of the factors defining organizational effectiveness, which leads to the conclusion that the most effective organizations are those that make the fewest mistakes in the way they hire and supervise their staff, recruit and train their managers, choose their strategy, and monitor the outcomes. Thus, every organization has its inefficiencies. As Pericles said to the elders of Athens on the eve of their war with Sparta, "I care less about the Spartans' strategy than I do about our mistakes."

6

The Psychology
of Managerial Incompetence

In this chapter, I describe the personality characteristics associated with managerial incompetence. I begin with two real-life examples to set the stage. I then describe some popular efforts to understand managerial incompetence. Finally, I outline the key research on the topic of derailment. Chapter 7 concerns ways to deal with flawed leadership.

THE KING OF UNDERWEAR

Harold Bright (not his real name), the disgraced CEO of a major underwear manufacturer, was a working-class boy who vowed to climb the corporate ladder. He is bright, charming, charismatic, and a master salesman; he is also a former athlete and fitness buff who once posed for an ad in his underwear; he banned cigarettes in the company and he would often start meetings with his managers by conducting calisthenics.

Mr. Bright acquired his company in 1985 in a leveraged buyout, and over the next 10 years, built its sales to $2 billion per year. As early as 1985, various business magazines described him as one of the richest men in America. He owned expensive homes in Colorado, Maine, and Chicago; he dated models and starlets; and in the process he married four times. He often mused out loud about running for president of the United States when he finished his business career. He ran the company like an emperor—he bought yachts, expensive artwork, and even a used MIG fighter plane. He also donated company money to charities and political candidates, and he personally controlled a portion of the company's pension fund investments, picking the stocks himself. He paid himself hugely—between 1996 and 1998 his salary was over $13 million per year, and one compensation firm described him as a perennial compensation abuser. Between 1994 and 1997, the company loaned him $103 million, which he used for personal business; he characterized these loans as perfectly normal, but they are not normal in a publicly held corporation. Bright also started a private company that consulted with his public company; between 1985 and 1996 his private company charged his underwear company more than $100 million in management fees.

In 1996, the company, facing stiff competition from other manufacturers, realized that its profits were dropping. Bright decided to move his manufacturing offshore; to raise some money, he went to Wall Street. Analysts promptly rallied behind him so that, in the spring of 1997, the company's stock was at an all-time high. At that point, Bright sold $39 million of his stock in the company, taking huge profits. In July 1997, Bright told Wall Street that company profits would not make expectations. By the end of the year, the company had lost $400 million, and a massive stock sell-off followed, as well as a class-action lawsuit by shareholders. Surprisingly, in early 1997 the Bank of America also gave Bright's company a $660 million revolving loan; by 1999, this loan had gone to zero. Nonetheless, in March 1999, still believing in Bright, a group of banks sold $250 million in public debt offering for the company. Shortly thereafter, the company announced a $9 million loss for the first quarter of 1999, and the price of the bonds collapsed. The company board fired Bright in August 1999, and then declared bankruptcy in December 1999. Although the company lost $576 million in 1999, Bright threatened legal action against the board; he blamed the directors and managers of the company for interfering with his plans for a recovery, and said the company owed him $100 million in severance and pension benefits. The key themes in this story are Bright's unusual charm and charisma, which disguised his massive selfishness, and profound sense of entitlement, which allowed him to claim compensation far beyond what was reasonable, and led him into a self-righteous rage when he was challenged.

CHAINSAW AL

Chainsaw Al Dunlap, a burly and aggressive West Point graduate, successfully improved the stock of four large U.S. corporations—American Can, Lily Tulip, Crown Zellerbach, and Scott Paper Company—by ruthlessly cutting costs and driving sales. At Scott Paper Company, for example, he increased share prices by 225% in 18 months, thereby improving the market value of the stock by $6.3 billion. Along the way, he acquired the nickname "Chainsaw Al" for his brutal management style, and came to describe himself as the best CEO in America. When he was hired to turn around the Sunbeam Corporation in late July 1996, Sunbeam shares went up 60%, to $18.60, based on Wall Street's expectations of his performance.

He began at Sunbeam as he had on previous occasions: He savagely and publicly denounced the inefficiency and incompetence of the former management, and he hired an accounting firm to justify the huge cuts in personnel and facilities that he wanted to make. Next, he made drastic cuts in staff and facilities—for example, he cut the Sunbeam human resources staff from 75 to 17 (most organizations have one HR person for every 100 employees, but after the cuts, Sunbeam had one HR person for every 300 employees). He then took a substantial one-time tax write-off worth $300 million. Finally, he gave his major managers stock options and then began putting "excruciating" pressure on them to increase sales.

In the first quarter of 1997 Sunbeam's earnings exceeded Wall Street's projections; in the second quarter, earnings met expectations; third quarter earnings again exceeded Wall Street projections, and Sunbeam stock hit its all-time record high of $50 per share. In the public sphere, everything looked rosy, but behind the scenes, things were rapidly deteriorating. First, by early 1997, Dunlap's leadership had stressed the management team to the breaking point.

Dunlap gave managers wildly unrealistic goals: They were required to double their total revenue, boost their operating margins from 2.5% to 20%, and generate $600 million in new product sales in 12 months. To make the sales volumes look good, products were heavily discounted; in other cases, products were shipped and billing was deferred until 1999. Dunlap's subordinates thought he wanted to drive the numbers quickly so that he could sell the business quickly, and he was repeatedly heard criticizing his banker for his inability to find a buyer.

Senior managers began to quit in 1997. In July 1997 one influential analyst downgraded the stock because Sunbeam's inventory was so high and cash reserves were so low. In addition, the rapid downsizing caused operational chaos and in some cases additional costs. Managers and employees were being fired every day and most departments and functions lacked the people to get a normal day's work done. Plants that were needed to produce goods already sold to retailers were shut down, and surviving factories lacked the parts needed to make their products. The accounting firm also recommended that Sunbeam fire its computer staff and outsource the entire IT function. Dunlap fired technicians who were making $35,000 per year and who quickly discovered they were worth $125,000 on the open market. To replace them, Sunbeam had to hire contract workers at a higher salary than the original workers, and in some cases had to rehire at a higher salary people who were just fired. Then Sunbeam tried to upgrade its computer systems with no backup. This resulted in their computers being down for months; clients such as Wal-Mart and Sears had to be invoiced manually.

By late fall 1997, things were desperate inside the organization; in the fourth quarter, the controller used $21.5 million in reserves (from the $300 million restructuring fee) to create income. This infusion covered a calamitous erosion in profit margins. On January 28th, 1998, Sunbeam reported earnings below Wall Street expectations, and the stock dropped almost 10%. The pressure to meet unreachable financial goals even got to Dunlap, who, in February, walked out on the golf course at the Boca Raton Resort and Golf Club, where he lived, and assaulted a passing golfer. In March 1998, an internal auditor wrote a memo complaining about a lack of prudent, ethical behavior … in order to "make numbers" for the company and resigned. On April 3, the chief of investor relations resigned. A Paine Webber analyst, who had always been suspicious of Dunlap's management practices, downgraded the stock, citing poor financial performance and high-level resignations, and the stock went into a free fall. Under pressure, Dunlap finally announced a first-quarter loss, and by the end of that day the stock lost 25% of its value. Dunlap's hand-picked board fired him on June 13. Finally given access to the books, they were appalled by the actual financial condition of the company, and shortly thereafter they filed for bankruptcy protection. By midyear the stock had fallen from $53 to $6 per share. The company lost $898 million in 1998, and Dunlap sued for $5.3 million in severance pay.

My sense is that Dunlap learned his leadership style in the military, where the standard practice is for a senior officer to be in a command for about 18 months, and future promotions depend on his or her making an impact in a short time span. This is typically done by driving the permanent staff of the command unmercifully, making some cosmetic improvements, and moving on, leaving behind a demoralized and embittered staff who the senior officer will never see again. The problem is that, in the military, there is rarely any financial accountability. The lessons that Dunlap learned in the military served him well in his first four CEO jobs—he was able to boost financial performance rapidly and then sell the company—but who knows at what cost to the organization he left behind.

THE BASE RATE OF FLAWED MANAGEMENT

In the early 1980s, I conducted a careful review of the empirical literature on leadership. I discovered that, other than such items as "leaders tend to be taller than their followers," there was very little convergence among researchers regarding the characteristics of effective leaders or managers. I decided it might be useful to turn the problem on its head and ask about the characteristics of bad or incompetent leaders. I was stimulated in this direction by Herzberg's (1966) musings on worker motivation. Herzberg interviewed a large number of accountants and engineers, and asked them what they liked best and least about their jobs. He found that their comments could be sorted into two categories, which he called hygiene factors and motivator factors. *Hygiene factors* are demotivators; they are factors that alienate workers. Removing these hygiene factors does not mean people will work harder, it means that they will not be demotivated. *Motivator factors* are motivators; their presence, Herzberg suggested, would lead to enhanced performance. What caught my attention, however, was Herzberg's detailed description of hygiene factors. A careful reading of his data showed quite clearly that by far the most important hygiene factor—or demotivator—was incompetent and abusive managers.

Climate surveys are a standard tool for guiding organizational development. Climate surveys are designed to reveal the mood of the workforce vis-à-vis the organization where they are employed. Climate surveys ask about worker satisfaction with pay, benefits, working conditions, safety, and so on. Climate surveys have been used with some regularity to study morale since World War II. A review of the climate survey literature reveals a very interesting generalization. It does not matter when the study is done—1948, 1958, 1968, 1998—it does not matter where the study is done—London, Baltimore, Seattle, Honolulu—and it does not matter what occupational group is studied—postal workers, milk truck drivers, school teachers—the results are always the same. About 75% of the workforce surveyed will say that the worst single aspect of their job, the most stressful aspect of their job, is their immediate supervisor.

In a related and little-known study, researchers at the Center for Creative Leadership in North Carolina conducted a series of interviews with a large number of managers about defining career events. Every one of them reported that he or she had spent a substantial amount of time working for an impossible boss—not difficult, cranky, picky, or abusive, but impossible. There are two conclusions from this study (McCall & Lombardo, 1983). The first is that every employed adult will have to work for a bad boss for some significant period of time. The second conclusion is that, when working for an intolerable boss, if a person tries to stick up for himself or herself and refuses to be bullied, his or her career will be irreparably damaged. When working for an awful boss, a person's only option is to suffer in silence. Putting this point differently, everyone will sooner or later have to work for an awful boss; those who fight back will lose; winners suffer in silence and see what they can learn from their bad boss regarding how not to manage others.

I then asked what the base rate (percentage) of incompetent management might be in the corporate world. Based on the results from all the climate surveys conducted over the years, and based on the research at the Center for Creative Leadership, I proposed that the base rate would be 65% to 75%; that is, 65% to 75% of existing managers are alienating their staff. The conventional wisdom in the occupational psychology community in the 1980s was that the base rate for managerial incompetence was 3% to 5%. I believed this estimate was self-serving and designed to flatter potential clients. David DeVries, former Executive Vice President of the Center for Creative Leadership in Greensboro, North Carolina, reported that, in his experience, about two thirds of all CEOs in the United States fail. Fernandez-Araoz (1999), in a *Harvard Business*

Review article, noted that "Between 30% and 50% of all executive-level appointments end in firing or resignation" (p. 109).

I would make three points about this question concerning the base rate of managerial incompetence. First, whatever the precise number might be, it is much larger than it needs to be. Meanwhile the current generation of bad managers are making the lives of their staffs miserable, as well as causing their organizations vast sums of unnecessary money in terms of absenteeism, turnover, bogus worker compensation claims, and outright sabotage as wronged workers try to retaliate. The U.S. Postal Service, for example, with more than 800,000 employees, has 150,000 labor grievances filed against it at any given time. The managers of the large postal service centers argue that if their workers are not filing grievances, they (the managers) are not doing their job—hence the concept of "going postal."

Second, the popular press carries evidence every day to support the claim that incompetent management is widespread. Consider, for example, an article in the *Washington Post* ("Out of Step with the Army," 2000). Young captains are leaving the U.S. Army after 5 to 10 years in record numbers. In 1989, at the end of the Cold War, 6.7% of Army captains left the service voluntarily. In 1999, 10.6% were leaving, a 58% increase. In 1989, 22% of junior officers surveyed said they intended to resign from the Army; in 1999, 50% said they intended to resign. These captains are the foundation of the Army's future management structure. Moreover, historically, officers have been more satisfied with the Army than enlisted troops; rising rates of officer dissatisfaction raise the possibility that enlisted retention, already a problem, may also be headed down. Army Chief of Staff General E. K. Shinseki commissioned a survey of 760 Army officers studying at the Command and General Staff College at Fort Leavenworth, Kansas. "The resulting reports, which have not been made public, are startling in their denunciations of the Army's current leadership," (Out of Step, 2000, p. 3). The report can be summarized as showing that the junior officers do not trust the senior leadership, that they feel senior officers will throw subordinates under the bus in a heartbeat to protect or advance their careers. The article raises the possibility that the resignation rate might reflect the allure of higher private sector wages, but participants in the study rejected this hypothesis; reflecting a widespread lack of faith in the Army's top generals, the respondents suggested that the entire senior leadership in the Army be replaced.

My third point is that I do not think that there are more incompetent managers around today than there were 30 or 50 years ago. Rather, I think people have become more aware of and more willing to talk about the problem, hopefully as a result of some of our earlier research. The awareness has been brought about by the increased use of climate surveys since World War II; climate surveys ask the workforce to evaluate management. The numbers come back the same, over and over, and eventually the message begins to penetrate popular consciousness.

The newfound awareness of the prevalence of incompetent managers in modern organizations has spawned a spate of analyses in the popular press. For example, in the *Harvard Business Review* article mentioned earlier, Fernandez-Araoz (1999) attributed the failure rate to flaws in the recruitment and selection process, and listed "Ten Deadly Traps" in the process:

- Trying to replicate the person who just left—always a bad idea.
- Not being clear what the job to be filled actually is.
- Choosing a candidate based on his or her response to your favorite question.
- Taking interview answers at face value.
- Believing the reports of references.
- Hiring someone just like you.
- Allowing junior people to run the hiring process.
- Hiring the person using an unstructured interview.
- Ignoring emotional intelligence (or trying to measure it with an interview).
- Members of the search committee hiring a weak candidate to enhance their own chances of getting ahead.

This is a sensible analysis even today—especially the implied critique of interviews as a method for hiring executives. One of my most important claims is that serious flaws of personality and character coexist quite nicely with excellent social skills. About the only thing an interview can evaluate is social skill. However, I disagree with the implicit claim that the high base rate of managerial incompetence in the corporate world can be explained by structural flaws in the hiring process. What is the explanation for the number of bad managers in the world of work? This is the question to which I now turn.

In my view, perhaps the most important contributor to this problem is the fact that nowhere in our educational system is there any systematic training for leadership. Competent leadership training does not occur in business schools, and it does not occur at the military academies—the Chainsaw Al anecdote and the *Washington Post* article suggest that military leadership is a near oxymoron. When the newly minted junior officer or MBA reports to his or her first duty assignment and is placed in charge of 15 to 50 staff members, what does he or she do? The new manager falls back on the lessons of the culture, which are enshrined in old John Wayne and Clint Eastwood movies. One great example here is a movie entitled *Twelve O'Clock High,* often described as a "board room classic" because it depicts the pressures of life at the top. In this World War II movie set in England, a U.S. bomber squadron is performing poorly. In the squadron, bombing "productivity" and morale are low, and casualties are high. The new commanding officer, played by Gregory Peck, attributes the poor performance to a lack of discipline—his predecessor was a worn-out wimp. Peck's character then begins whipping his new command into shape, and he gets his bombing numbers up by driving his staff mercilessly. He is, of course, hated, and only later does his staff begin to appreciate his effectiveness. The moral of the movie is that leadership is a dirty job, but someone has to do it for the sake of the war effort. Young people are raised on a diet of such material, which portrays badly flawed leadership tactics as admirable, and they unconsciously fall back on these models when they themselves assume leadership positions. Specifically, the models of leadership portrayed in popular culture are overwhelmingly wrongheaded, but they are the models that prevail, and this is a partial explanation for the base rate problem.

MODELS OF BAD MANAGEMENT

The widespread prevalence of bad management has led to a spate of analyses in the popular press. I mention two for illustrative purposes. For example, an article by Waldroop and Butler (1998) in *Fortune* lists "Eight Failings That Bedevil the Best." The article suggests that managers fail for eight characteristic and recurring reasons that can be classified as follows:

1. *Home-run hitters* are persons who go directly into business after graduate business school, without gaining any real-world business experience, and fail. They fail because they want to make their fortunes immediately and do not know enough about business to know what they do not know, a recipe for disaster.

2. *Early harvesters* are persons who, after graduate business school and a brief amount of business experience, decide it is time for their big payday. They have an exaggerated sense of their market value, begin making exorbitant salary demands, and soon find themselves unemployed.

3. *Meritocrats* are people who retain an A-student mentality even after they are employed. This results in a tendency to work hard to find the right answers, but an indifference to the process of selling the answers within the organization once they have been discovered. The result is an alienated "smarty pants," a bright and technically competent person whose future is doomed by his or her self-righteous unwillingness to play necessary corporate politics.

4. *Peacekeepers* are people who are overly concerned with maintaining harmonious relations with others. Their dislike of confrontations and their unwillingness to fight for their views inevitably undermines their effectiveness.

5. *Heroes* are characterized by two characteristics: (a) a willingness to go through a brick wall to complete a project—even when there is an open door available, and (b) a need to be completely in control, which leads to micromanagement and staff alienation.

6. *Rebels* are persons who insist on doing things their way, on being themselves, regardless of the corporate culture that surrounds them. This entails dressing differently, offering unusual and unsolicited opinions, and violating a large number of implicit rules and norms on the grounds that they are being authentic.

7. *Mr. Spocks* are persons who are bright and technically competent, but who ignore the human and political implications of their decisions and actions. Despite the validity of their decisions, they build a base of enemies whose input they ignore, and the resistance of their enemies inevitably defeats them.

8. *Acrophobes* are persons who doubt that they deserve the success they have achieved; they feel like fakers or poseurs, masquerading as senior managers. Unless they are able to manage their feelings of inadequacy, they do self-defeating things that ensure their own failure.

This list of categories of failure is clearly ad hoc, but it contains four themes that are valid. First, home-run hitters and early harvesters are characterized by an exaggerated sense of entitlement, and that is, in fact, a problem for many modern managers. Second, meritocrats, rebels, and Spocks are characterized by a lack of awareness about or indifference to the way others are reacting to them, and this is also a problem for many managers. Third, peacekeepers are characterized by an exaggerated need for approval and social support, which is a real theme. Finally, the acrophobe is characterized by insecurity and low self-confidence, and this is also a theme in the careers of some failed managers.

Another example of the popular interest in bad management is another article in the *Fortune* magazine (Charan & Colvin, 1999). The article, entitled "Why CEOs Fail," begins by presenting an imposing list of CEOs who were fired from major corporations over the preceding 5 years. The authors then presented a case-by-case analysis of the reasons why these CEOs failed. They noted at the outset that all the failed CEOs are intelligent, articulate, dedicated, and the sort of persons who would get high marks in an executive assessment center or at a recruiting firm. The authors argued that CEOs fail for one common and obvious reason—poor execution and an inability to deliver on commitments. In short, they could not get things done. I return to this topic at the end of the chapter.

The, next question is why the CEOs could not get anything done, and the bulk of their article concerns listing the reasons. They proposed five. The first is what they called bad staffing decisions, which involves recruiting and appointing the wrong people, then sticking with them when the evidence is clear that they are not performing up to standards. This is a specific example of the more general problem that plagues all bad managers—an inability to build and maintain a high-performing team.

The second reason managers cannot get anything done, according to Charan and Colvin (1999), is what they called *process gridlock*. They meant by this an inability to make timely decisions. This may reflect the fact that the CEO is personally indecisive, or that he or she is wedded to a decision-making process that is slow, insular, and unresponsive. Either way, the result is gridlock, subordinate frustration, and corporate failure.

The third reason CEOs fail, in this popular analysis, is that they do not hold people accountable for their performance. As psychologists, we should ask why CEOs fail to hold their staff accountable. A variety of reasons spring to mind: The CEO is disorganized and cannot keep track, the CEO lacks the self-discipline needed to engage in systematic follow-up, or the CEO dislikes confrontations and making people feel uncomfortable.

A fourth reason CEOs fail, in this model, is that they do not derive, or have stopped deriving, enjoyment from making things go better in their organizations. An important task of leadership is pushing for continuous improvement. When CEOs are no longer concerned about this, they have lost focus and the organization will begin to dwindle or drift.

Finally, CEOs get in trouble when they begin to ignore market realities—when market share, profit margins, and stock prices begin to decline and the CEO is perceived as indifferent or unresponsive to these realities. Again, the question is, why would a CEO ignore market realities? This might reflect arrogance, or burnout, or self-deception, or denial, but as Freud warned us long ago, when reality testing fails, dysfunctional behavior soon appears.

It follows from this analysis, and data support these conclusions, that successful CEOs make good staffing decisions, make timely decisions, hold people accountable, take pleasure in continuously improving organizational processes, and have a clear sense of market realities. These generalizations are true, but they are essentially descriptive and cry out for further analysis.

STUDIES OF FAILED MANAGERS

Going forward in this chapter, we are moving in a direction of increasing analytical rigor, so it might be appropriate to define more carefully what I mean by managerial failure. Failure concerns being involuntarily plateaued, demoted, or fired before a manager reaches his or her anticipated level of achievement, or after reaching that level unexpectedly failing. Middle- and upper level derailment has been only infrequently studied in a careful, rigorous, and scientific way. Traditionally, failure has been attributed to having less or fewer of the characteristics associated with success (see Table 6.1; cf. Boyatzis, 1982), such as leadership skills, administrative talent, ability to form relationships, and so on. I suggest that high-level failure is more a function of having something undesirable than lacking something desirable.

V. Jon Bentz, Vice President for Human Resources at Sears in the 1970s, was the first person to do a systematic study of managerial failure. Managers at Sears were hired using a well-validated executive assessment battery (Bentz, 1967), ensuring that entry-level managers were bright, confident, energetic, and socially skilled. Nonetheless, well over half of them failed, raising the possibility, only hinted at earlier, that management failure is not a function of lacking some general feature of leadership such as social skill. Rather, failure seems to be associated with having something in addition to the normally expected attributes of a manager, something that actively contributes to a person's failure.

Table 6.1
Why U.S. Presidents Fail

1. Poor public speaking skills (Gerald Ford, George Bush).
2. Organizational inexperience (John Kennedy before the Bay of Pigs).
3. Unable to build relationships with a wide range of potential supporters (Jimmy Carter).
4. Unfocused policy vision (Lyndon Johnson on the Vietnam war).
5. No strategic intelligence (Jimmy Carter's "obsessive attention to detail").
6. No emotional intelligence (Lyndon Johnson's temper, Richard Nixon's paranoia, Jimmy Carter's rigidity, Bill Clinton's lack of self-discipline).

Bentz (1990) conducted interviews with a large sample of failed Sears executives and tried to determine why they derailed. Bentz, a courtly, perceptive man and a skilled interviewer, studied his notes, formed categories of recurring tendencies, and then summarized his findings in terms of seven themes. Each of these themes was masked or covered over by a strong personality:

1. A lack of administrative skill—for example, knowing how to delegate or prioritize.
2. A failure to shape events by being reactive rather than proactive.
3. An inability to deal with the scope and scale of a large organization—for example, failure to coordinate actions with others or an inability to maintain relationships with an extended staff.
4. A failure to provide leadership—for example, did not build a team.
5. Poor judgment caused by being overly emotional or intellectually limited.
6. An insufficient knowledge of the business—probably associated with being a slow learner.
7. An overriding personality defect (this is a grab-bag category that includes being volatile, insensitive, cold, arrogant, overly emotional, or lacking composure).

In a second study, reported at about the same time, McCall and Lombardo (1983) also interviewed a group of executives who had derailed. They analyzed their interview data and placed the causes of failure in 12 categories that obviously parallel Bentz's findings. Again, each of these tendencies is masked by a strong personality—which is why the person was hired.

1. Specific performance problems (inability to handle certain kinds of jobs).
2. Social insensitivity (being abusive, abrasive, intimidating, or a bully).
3. Being cold, aloof, or arrogant.
4. Betrayal of trust.
5. Overmanaging, undermanaging, failing to delegate or to build a team.
6. Being overly ambitious (playing politics and thinking about the next job).
7. Not staffing effectively.
8. Inability to think strategically.
9. Inability to adapt to his or her boss.
10. Overly dependent on an earlier sponsor or mentor.
11. Specific skill deficiencies (which will depend on the job).
12. Burned out.

In a subsequent and substantially more rigorous piece of research, Lombardo, Ruderman, and McCauley (1987) obtained ratings for 169 mid- to upper level managers in a multinational food and beverage company. The managers were rated on a set of items developed from several quantitative studies of more than 400 executives from several organizations, and the items concerned skills, attitudes, values, and derailment factors. They grouped these items into eight categories. In the sample of 169 managers, 83 had derailed. All were rated, and the derailed managers were significantly different from the successful managers across all categories. These categories are listed here, along with the specific item that best defines the category.

1. Handling business complexity: "Is a source of good ideas." (Derailed managers are not a source of good ideas.)
2. Directing, motivating, and developing subordinates: "Coaches and develops subordinates by giving feedback and providing a challenging climate and opportunity." (Derailed managers do not do this.)
3. Integrity: "Is loyal to the company." (Derailed mangers are often disloyal.)
4. Drive for excellence: "Has good track record."

5. Organizational savvy: "Knows politics are very much a part of organizational life and must be taken into account if you are to get things done."
6. Composure: "Is emotionally stable and predictable".
7. Sensitivity: "Can get along with all kinds of people".
8. Staffing: "Recruits and hires good people."

Once again, the important point is that the derailed managers were hired on the basis of their strong personalities and the eight types of problems just listed emerged only after prolonged exposure to them. Table 6.2 summarizes and compares the results of the three studies just reviewed. As you will quickly see, there is substantial overlap in the results. These three studies form the basic background for our thinking and research on managerial derailment, the topic to which I now turn.

THE PERSONALITY DISORDERS

In professional as opposed to popular psychology, there are two very different ways of thinking about the origins of problematic behavior. The first model, which is most dramatically exemplified by Freud, is the intrapsychic tradition. Freud argued that most people are crippled by anxiety, guilt, depression, and low self-esteem. The cause of the anxiety and so on comes from one's relations with one's parents and caretakers in childhood, and the solution to these problems comes from discovering lost memories—traumatic events that are buried in a person's unconscious. This model prevailed throughout most of the 20th century. There are two primary problems with this traditional, intrapsychic model. On the one hand, anxiety and depression can be, and often are, treated with mood-altering drugs, thereby raising a question about the utility of exploring the unconscious. On the other hand, there are many people with terrible behavior problems but with no anxiety, guilt, or depression—drug addicts and criminals are powerful examples of this generalization.

The second tradition is less well known, less dramatic, and inherently less interesting, but may be more valid; it is the interpersonal tradition as exemplified by a group of American writers—H. S. Sullivan, Timothy Leary, George Kelly, Robert Carson, and Jerry Wiggins—and their "students"—Lorna Benjamin and Donald Kiesler. These writers focus on the causes of interpersonal behavior, rather than the causes of anxiety and depression. They argue that the causes of flawed inter-

Table 6.2

Comparative Results of Three Studies of Managerial Derailment

Bentz	McCall & Lombardo (1983)	Lombardo, Ruderman, & McCauley (1987)
Lack of business knowledge	Specific business problems	Handling business complexity
Lack of business skill	Unable to think strategically	
Failure of leadership	Over-and undermanaging	Directing, motivating, and developing subordinates
	Not staffing effectively	
Failure to shape events	Specific performance problems	Drive for excellence
Lack of administrative skill	Overly ambitious	savvy
Poor judgment	Social insensitivity	Sensitivity
Overriding personality defect		
Inability to deal with scop and scale	Failing to staff effectively	Staffing

personal behavior are not buried, unconscious memories, but wrong-headed theories about what other people expect of you. We all develop theories about the world, including theories about other people, and we use these theories to guide our behavior. Some people have more adequate theories than others—theories that lead to more accurate predictions of others' responses. Some people are more willing to change, refine, and upgrade their theories than other people are. On the one hand, interpersonal theory is certainly correct: We do in fact do what is on our minds; our interpersonal behavior is definitely theory driven. On the other hand, it is very hard to measure these theories or deal with them in a rigorous manner.

In my view, these two traditions are not in competition because they concern different kinds of problems. Intrapsychic theory concerns problems that usually develop in the first 3 years of life and learning to live with oneself. Interpersonal theory concerns problems that usually develop after a child begins school and learning to live with others. In my view, the problems that cause managers to derail are typically in the interpersonal rather than the intrapsychic domain. Problematic managers are typically quite happy with themselves, and they attribute their occupational problems to other people.

In the 1970s, psychologists and psychiatrists became increasingly interested in what are called *personality disorders,* dysfunctional dispositions that may or may not be associated with anxiety and depression—the traditional indicators of neuroticism—but that are associated with poor social and occupational performance. In reading the research on managerial derailment described previously, I was immediately struck by the parallels between the dimensions uncovered by Bentz, McCall, and Lombardo and the standard personality disorders, listed in Table 6.3.

From the perspective of interpersonal theory, people have problems with other people when they organize their lives on the basis of ideas that are inappropriate for their circumstances. For example, I recently worked with a manager who was having problems adjusting at work. He is bright, ambitious, and pleasant, but he is a poor team player who persistently competes with his colleagues and constantly calls attention to himself. After some analysis, it turns out that he was the youngest of several boys in an affluent family that stressed achievement and high performance. It was clear to us that he brought to his career the methods he had refined in childhood that allowed him to compete with his older and very successful brothers. In short, he was conducting his adult life in terms of a set of rules and strategies that were appropriate to earlier

TABLE 6.3

Standard Personality Disorders

Disorder	Description
Borderline	Inappropriate anger, unstable and intense relationships alternating between idealization and devaluation.
Paranoid	Distrustful and suspicious of others; motives are interpreted as malevolent.
Avoidant	Social inhibition, feelings of inadequacy, and hypersensitivity to criticism or rejection.
Schizoid	Emotional coldness and detachment from social relationships; indifference to praise and criticism.
Passive-aggressive	Passive resistance to adequate social and occupational performance; irritation when asked to do something he or she does not want to do.
Narcissism	Arrogant and haughty behaviors or attitudes; grandiose sense of self-importance and entitlement.
Antisocial	Disregard for the truth; impulsivity and failure to plan ahead; failure to conform with social norms.
Histrionic	Excessive emotionality and attention seeking; self-dramatizing, theatrical, and exaggerated emotional expression.
Schizotypal	Odd beliefs or magical thinking; behavior or speech that is odd, eccentric, or peculiar.
Obsessive-compulsive	Preoccupations with orderliness, rules, perfectionism, and control; overconscientious and inflexible.
Dependent	Difficulty making everyday decisions without excessive advice and reassurance; difficulty expressing disagreement out of fear of loss of support or approval.

life circumstances, but that were now inappropriate. This is what I mean by personality disorders—using interpersonal strategies that are no longer functional. Once again, I think of the standard taxonomy of personality disorders as an effort to classify and organize the behavioral consequences of flawed interpersonal strategies.

In the late 1980s, as an academic exercise, I began to develop measures for the 11 most common personality disorders. In 1992 I gathered some data on the relation between these measures and actual job performance in a large insurance company; again, however, this was a purely academic exercise. To my genuine surprise, these 11 scales were steadily and consistently related to job performance in a variety of job categories. At that point I began to take the measure seriously and in 1997 we published the first version of what we call the Hogan Development Survey (HDS; Hogan & Hogan, 1997). We subsequently have used the HDS to give developmental feedback to several thousand managers and executives in a number of large organizations. I next describe the 11 dimensions of the HDS and their implications for leadership performance.

Excitable

Persons with high scores on this dimension expect to be disappointed in relationships; they anticipate being rejected, ignored, criticized, cheated, or treated unfairly. As a result, they are very much on guard for signs that others have or will treat them badly. When they think they have been mistreated, they erupt in emotional displays that may involve yelling, throwing things, and slamming doors. Because they are so alert for signs of mistreatment, they find them everywhere, even when others cannot see them. From the observer's perspective, what is most distinctive about these people is their emotional eruptions; they are the people for whom the term *emotional intelligence* was devised. The two fundamental dimensions of interpersonal appraisal concern being predictable and being rewarding to deal with; these people are unpredictable—you never know when they are going to erupt—and they are unrewarding because they are so edgy and self-centered. As a result of their unpredictability and unrewardingness, they have a lot of trouble building and maintaining a team—the fundamental task of leadership.

At their best, these people are sensitive to the plight of others; they have a great capacity for empathy; because they know that life is not always fair, they can genuinely feel others' pain. They also tend to be enthusiastic about, and to work very hard on, new projects—they bring a sense of energy and urgency to new projects. At their worst, however, they are high maintenance—they require a lot of hand holding and reassurance, and they are very hard to please.

These people do not handle stress, failure, or disappointment very well, and they tend to "melt down" rather easily. In addition, they are hard people with whom to talk and maintain a relationship. As a result, they change jobs frequently and they have a large number of failed relationships; this is because, in the history of their relationships, they are so easily disappointed, and when disappointed, their first instinct is to withdraw and leave. A key feature of these people, which others may rarely see, is that they are extremely self-centered—all information and experience is evaluated in terms of what it means for them personally—and they take every comment, gesture, and expression of others personally. They personalize everything, but they do so privately; what others see are the emotional outbursts and the tendency to withdraw.

To work with these people, you must be prepared to provide them with a lot of reassurance, keep them well informed to minimize surprises, and give them a lot of previews so they know what is coming. The general model for handling them is one of trying to soothe a fretful child.

Skeptical

Persons with high scores on this dimension expect to be wronged, betrayed, set up, cheated, or deceived in some way. They see the world as a dangerous place, full of potential enemies, and they specialize in conspiracy theories. Consequently, they are keenly alert for signs of having been mistreated, and when they think it has happened, they retaliate openly and directly. This may involve physical violence, accusations, retaliation, or litigation, and the retaliation is designed to send the signal that they are prepared to defend themselves. Because they are so alert for signs of betrayal, they inevitably find some, even though others might not see it, and when they find it, they take direct action. From the observer's perspective, what is most distinctive about these people is their suspiciousness, their argumentativeness, and their lack of trust in others. They are hard to deal with on a continuing basis because you never know when they are going to be offended by something (unpredictability), and because they are so focused on their own private agenda they do not have much time for others (unrewarding).

These people are typically bright, thoughtful, and perceptive, and have complex but well-worked-out theories of the world. Their theories are so well developed that they can interpret virtually anything with them, and the interpretations will make sense intellectually. At their best they are very insightful about organizational politics and the motives of their counter players, and they can be the source of very good intelligence regarding the real agendas of others, and the real meaning of events. Although they are very insightful about politics, they are often not very good at playing politics. This is because they are true believers, they are deeply committed to their worldview, and they tend to be unwilling to compromise, even on small issues. Nonetheless, with their passionate commitment to a theory about how the world works, they can be visionary and charismatic, and people may be drawn to them. Perhaps the best example of this in the 20th century was Adolph Hitler, but other examples, including Joseph Stalin and Saddam Hussein, come quickly to mind. Because they are unpredictable and not rewarding to deal with, these people have trouble maintaining relationships or teams over a long time period.

These people handle stress by going to the bunkers, by withdrawing into their ideology and then attacking what is threatening them. They are very persistent, and will not give up without a fight. Over time, they tend to accumulate enemies, so there is a self-fulfilling quality to their lifestyles. They are self-centered and ideology centered—all information and experience is filtered through their worldview and evaluated in terms of the degree to which it fits with or threatens that view, which somehow reflects on them.

To work with these people, you have no alternative but to agree with them. If you disagree with them and then try to persuade them that they are wrong on an issue, they will defeat your objections in a way that makes sense to them. You will not be able to persuade them that they are wrong, and you risk alienating them by challenging them. Once they decide you cannot be trusted, the relationship will be over, and you will join the ranks of their many enemies, because you are either for them or against them.

Cautious

Persons with high scores on this dimension fear being criticized, shamed, blamed, humiliated, or somehow disgraced. They do not handle failure, rejection, or criticism well; as a result, they are constantly on guard against the possibilities of making errors, mistakes, blunders, or missteps that might cause them to be criticized and publicly embarrassed. Because they are so alert to possible criticism, they see hazards and threats everywhere, even when others cannot see them. They respond to the possibility of being criticized by hand wringing, perseveration, freezing, becoming very cautious, and taking no action at all. Their cautiousness extends to their staff, whom they fear will do something to embarrass them. Consequently, they tend to forbid their staff from taking any initiative. These people are unpopular managers because they are so cautious, indecisive, and controlling.

At their best, these people are prudent, careful, and meticulous about evaluating risk; they rarely make rash or ill-advised moves, and they provide sound, prudential advice about intended future courses of action. They make a good counterfoil to impulsive, entrepreneurial types who tend to go off half cocked. At their worst, however, they avoid innovation, resist change, and stall and drag their feet, even when it is apparent that something needs to be done. They seem particularly threatened by the new, the different, and the strange, and they vastly prefer to react rather than take initiative.

Under pressure, stress, and heavy workloads they begin to adhere religiously to established procedures, and will rely on the tried and true rather than on any new technology or other procedures. Most important, they will begin carefully to control their staff, in fear that someone will make a mistake and embarrass them, especially with their seniors. Under pressure, these people resemble the classic authoritarian personalities—they do exactly what their seniors tell them and they enforce standard rules and procedures on their staff and others over whom they have any power. They hate to be criticized; what others will see is cautiousness, rigidity, adherence to standardized procedures, and resistance to innovation and change.

To work with these people, you need to keep them well informed about any activities that concern them—where negative outcomes could reflect on them—and to consult them about your intended future actions. When rapid action is needed, or when some form of innovation needs to be implemented, it is best to go around them if that is possible. If it is not possible, then put in writing the fact that you recommended action or innovation, then be prepared for nothing to happen.

Reserved

Persons with high scores on this dimension seem self-absorbed, self-focused, indifferent to the feelings or opinions of others—especially their staff—introverted, misanthropic, imperceptive, and lacking in social insight. They seem thick skinned and impervious to rejection or criticism. They prefer to work alone, and are more interested in data and things than in people. They tend to work in finance, accounting, programming, and information technology where their progress will depend on their technical skills and not their social insight. These people are incommunicative and insensitive, which makes them unpredictable and unrewarding to deal with, and they have trouble building or maintaining a team.

At their best, these people are very tough in the face of political adversity; they have a hard carapace, and they can take criticism, rejection, and opprobrium where fainter hearts would tremble. They can also stay focused and on task, and not be distracted by tumult, emotional upheavals, and stressful meetings; through it all, they will continue to do their jobs. At their worst, however, they are insensitive to others' needs, moods, or feelings, and can be rude, tactless, imperceptive, and gauche.

These people are unperturbed by stress and heavy workloads; at the same time, they are insensitive or indifferent to the stress levels of their staff. When the pressure is really on, these people retreat into their offices, begin handling matters themselves, and stop communicating, which leaves others at a loss to know what they want or need. Again, these people are extremely self-centered and self-reliant; they do not need emotional support from others, and they do not provide any to others. They primarily do not want to be bothered by other peoples' problems, they just want to do their work.

To work with these people, you should stay task oriented and keep questions and comments job related. They will ignore requests for more and better communications, and will tend to work by themselves. You can do two things in response. First, observe what they do so that you do not act that way yourself. Second, develop lines of communication to other people in the organization so that you will have a source of advice during times of trouble.

Leisurely

Persons with high scores on this dimension march to the sound of their own drum. They are confident about their skills and abilities, cynical about the talents and intentions of others—especially superiors—and they insist on working at their own pace. When pressed for additional output, they get angry and slow down even more. They tend to feel mistreated, unappreciated, and put upon, and they are keenly sensitive to signs of disrespect. When they sense that they have been cheated or disrespected, they retaliate, but always under conditions of high deniability. They are often quite skilled in an interpersonal sense, they are good at hiding their annoyance and pretending to be cooperative, and their peevishness and foot dragging are often very hard to detect.

From an observer's perspective, what is most distinctive about these people is the fact that they are always late for meetings, they procrastinate, they work at about 80% of their capacity, and they are very stubborn and hard to coach. Their particular specialty, however, is the way they treat comments and suggestions by others: There will be an eyebrow flash, a slight smirk, a subtle shake of the head indicating disagreement, then a clever comment or argument that reveals how naive or stupid they thought the suggestion actually was. However, there will rarely be a direct confrontation. Their prickly sensitivity, subtle uncooperativeness, stubbornness, and deep self-absorption make them both unpredictable and unrewarding to deal with. As a result, they have trouble building and maintaining a team.

These people handle stress and heavy workloads by slowing down, ignoring requests for greater output, and finding ways to get out of work. Again, however, they have excellent social skills, they seem overtly cooperative and agreeable, and it takes a long time to realize how unproductive and refractory they actually are. A key to understanding these people is that they are quite self-centered, they focus on their own agendas, and they deeply believe in their own superior natural talent. As a result, they have nothing to prove to themselves, and they are quite indifferent to feedback from others. This is, of course, why they become so annoyed and resentful when criticized or asked for extra effort.

There are two keys to working with these people. First, you need to be aware that they are not nearly as cooperative as they seem, and that they are only pretending to agree with you about work and performance issues. Second, you need to get them to commit to performance goals in public, in front of witnesses, so that a community of people can hold them accountable. Social pressure will not change their views of the world, but it will serve to make their performance deficits harder to deny.

Bold

Clinical psychologists interpret the psychology of the narcissist using the metaphor of "the lord of the high chair." Imagine an indulged 2-year-old, sitting in his or her high chair; banging implements on his or her tray; demanding food, drink, and attention; and squealing in fury when his or her needs are not met. Now imagine that 2-year-old as an adult, but with his or her fundamental psychology still intact, and that is a narcissist. Persons with high scores on this dimension expect to be liked, admired, respected, attended to, praised, complimented, and indulged. Their most important characteristics are a sense of entitlement, excessive self-esteem, and an expectation of success that, as

Freud said, often leads to real success. They expect to be successful at everything they undertake, they believe that books will be written about them, and when their needs and expectations are frustrated, they explode with narcissistic rage. Clinical psychologists think the rage reveals underlying insecurity, but I think it reveals exaggerated expectations of what they are due.

From the observer's perspective, what is most distinctive about these people is their self-assurance, which often gives them a certain charisma—they are the first to speak in a group, and they hold forth with great confidence, even when they are wrong. A standard description of these people is "frequently in error but never in doubt." They often test the limits of what is permissible because they so completely expect to succeed. They take more credit for success than is warranted or fair, and they refuse to acknowledge failure, errors, or mistakes. When things go right, it is because of their efforts; when things go wrong, it is someone else's fault. This leads to problems with truth telling because they spin compulsively, and quickly reinterpret their failures and mistakes, usually by blaming them on others.

At their best, these people are energetic, charismatic, leaderlike, and willing to take the initiative to get projects moving. They are fearless about taking on truly daunting tasks, such as running for president of the United States. Success in management, sales, and entrepreneurship requires some elevation on this dimension. At their worst, however, they are arrogant, vain, overbearing, demanding, self-deceived, and pompous. Because they are so colorful and engaging, they often attract followers. However, because they are mercurial and abusive, they also soon alienate followers.

These people handle stress and heavy workloads with ease, they are quite persistent under pressure, and they refuse to acknowledge failure. Eisenhower's description of Field Marshal Montgomery comes to mind here: "Indomitable in defeat, insufferable in victory." Failure is always externalized and attributed to other causes. As a result of their inability to acknowledge failure or even mistakes and the way they resist coaching and ignore negative feedback, they are unable to learn from experience.

To work with these people, you must be prepared to flatter them, agree with them, exploited, allow them to take credit for your accomplishments, and allow them to blame you for their failures. Along the way, however, you will profit from observing their pluck, stamina, and ability to manipulate others to achieve their ends.

Mischievous

Persons with high scores on this dimension expect that others will like them and find them charming; consequently, they expect to be able to extract favors, promises, money, and other resources from other people with relative ease. They see others as utilities to be exploited, and therefore have problems maintaining commitments, and are unconcerned about violating expectations. They are self-confident to the point of feeling invulnerable, and have an air of daring and *sang froid* that others often find attractive and even irresistible—think of bullfighters, fighter pilots, race car drivers, or the English poet George Gordon, Lord Byron, the rakish role model for young men for a century.

From the observer's perspective, what is most distinctive about these people is their charm, their self-assurance, their verbal facility, and the sort of flirtatiousness one sees in cats—coyness, independence, and a willingness to favor you with their attention should you be so lucky. These people are highly rewarding to deal with, but they are also quite unpredictable. At their best, they are charming, fun, engaging, courageous, and somewhat seductive; at their worst, they are impulsive, reckless, faithless, remorseless, and exploitative. They also have problems with truth telling; they are quite manipulative and think they can talk their way out of any problem. The great American architect, Frank Lloyd Wright, was said to be a compulsive liar; sometimes he would lie to get a project, sometimes he would lie to save a project, and sometimes he would lie for the sheer joy of lying. Their self-deception, self-confidence, and recklessness will create lots of conflicts, but they have almost no ability to learn from experience. They tend to be underachievers, relative to their talent and capabilities; this is due to their impulsiveness, their recklessness, and their inability to admit they have made a mistake.

These people handle stress and heavy workloads with great aplomb. They are easily bored, and find stress, danger, and risk to be invigorating—they actively seek it. As a result, many of these people become heroes: They intervene in robberies, rush into burning buildings, take apart live bombs, volunteer for dangerous assignments, and flourish in times of war and chaos. Conversely, they adapt poorly to the requirements of structured bureaucracies.

To work with these people, you must be prepared to fill in behind them, to help them follow through with commitments and pay attention to details, and to encourage them to think through the consequences of their actions. At the same time, you should not expect a lot of gratitude or even loyalty. Nonetheless, you can learn a lot by watching how they handle people and how they are able to get what they want through charm and persuasion.

Colorful

Persons with high scores on this dimension believe that others will find them interesting, engaging, and worth paying attention to. They are good at calling attention to themselves—they know how to make dramatic entrances and exits, they carry themselves with flair, and self-consciously pay attention to their clothes and to the way others react to them. Some elevation on this scale is essential for a career in sales, politics, or the theater. A prototype of this dimension is Winston Churchill, the great British statesman of the 1930s and 1940s, who gave stirring speeches, and using a variety of stage props, cultivated a vivid public personality and generally was *una bella figura*. He also saved England from Hitler and changed the course of world history.

From an observer's perspective, what is most distinctive about these people is their stage presence or persona and their self-conscious and distinctive aura—they perform extremely well in interviews, in assessment centers, and other public settings. They are great fun to watch, but they are also impulsive and unpredictable; everything that makes them good at sales (and selling themselves) makes them poor managers: They are noisy, easily distracted, overcommitted, and love to be the center of attention. They are not necessarily extroverted; they are just good at calling attention to themselves. At their best, they are bright, colorful, entertaining, fun, flirtatious, and the life of the party. At their worst, they do not listen, they do not plan, they self-nominate and self-promote, and they ignore negative feedback.

These people deal with stress and heavy workloads by becoming very busy; they enjoy high pressure and high-drama situations because they can then be the star. When they come into a room, one has the sense that a fan has been turned on, and papers begin flying about. Breathless with excitement, they confuse activity with productivity and evaluate themselves in terms of how many meetings they attend rather than how much they actually get done. A key feature of these people that others may not appreciate is how much they need and feed off of approval, and how hard they are willing to work for it. This explains why they persist in trying to be a star long after their luster has faded.

To work with these people, one has to be prepared to put up with missed appointments, bad organization, rapid change of direction, and indecisiveness. These matters will never change, although they can be planned for. At the same time, by watching them you can learn how to read social cues; learn how to present your views effectively, forcefully, and dramatically; and learn how to flatter and dazzle other people.

Imaginative

Persons with high scores on this dimension think about the world in unusual and often quite interesting ways, and they enjoy entertaining others with their unusual perceptions and insights. They are constantly alert to new ways of seeing, thinking, and expressing themselves, and they enjoy the reactions they are able to elicit in other people with their unusual forms of self-expression. From the observer's perspective, these people often seem bright, colorful, insightful, imaginative, very playful, and innovative, but also eccentric, odd, and flighty. A prototype for this kind of person is Sir Elton John, the British rock star, playing a piano in Wembley Stadium, dressed in a chicken suit.

These people are very interesting and fun to be around, but they are easily distracted and unpredictable and as managers they often leave people confused regarding their directions or intentions. People are confused in part because their directions change so quickly, but they are also confused because these people tend to communicate in idiosyncratic and unusual ways. At their best, these people are imaginative, creative, interesting, and amazingly insightful about the motives of others. At their worst, they can be self-absorbed, single-minded, insensitive to the reactions of others, and indifferent to the social and political consequences of their single-minded focus on their own agendas.

Under stress and heavy workloads, these people can become upset, lose focus, lapse into eccentric behavior, and not communicate clearly. They can also be moody and tend to get too excited by success and too despondent over failure. A key feature of these people that others may not appreciate is the degree to which they want attention, approval, and applause, which explains the lengths to which they are willing to attract it. In an airport, watch for purple hair, exotic tattoos, chartreuse suits, and flamboyant costumes—these are some telltale marks of these people.

To work with these people, one needs primarily to be a good audience; to appreciate their humor, creativity, and spontaneity, and to understand that they do not handle reversals very well. They are easily distracted and not very bottom-line oriented, and they are not arrogant; therefore they will not mind suggestions and recommendations regarding important decisions, and in fact may even appreciate them. Meanwhile, you should study their problem-solving style, listen to their insights about other people, and model their ability to think outside the lines.

Diligent

Persons with high scores on this dimension are concerned with doing a good job, being a good citizen, and pleasing authority. They are hard working, careful, planful, meticulous, and have very high standards of performance for themselves and other people. They live by these rules and they expect others to do so, so they become irritable when others do not follow their rules. From the observer's perspective, what is most distinctive about these people is their conservatism, their detail orientation, their risk aversion, but also the degree to which they are reliable, dependable, and predictable. They are marvelous organizational citizens who can be relied on to maintain standards, do their work competently and professionally, and treat their colleagues with respect.

At their best, these people are good role models who uphold the highest standards of professionalism in performance and comportment; they are typically very popular with their bosses because they are so completely reliable. At their worst, however, they are fussy, particular, nitpicking micromanagers who deprive their subordinates of any choice or control over their work. The micromanagement alienates their staff, who soon refuse to take any initiative and simply wait to be told what to do and how to do it. These people also cause a lot of stress for themselves; their obsessive concern for quality and high performance makes it difficult for them to delegate—"If you want something done right, you need to do it yourself." It also makes it difficult for them to prioritize their tasks—"If something is worth doing, it is worth doing well." They also have problems with vision and the big picture—"If you pay attention to details, the big picture will take care of itself." Consequently, they have a kind of ambivalent status as managers. Their superiors love them because they are so reliable. Their staff will appreciate how predictable they are, but their inability to delegate and their lack of interest in a vision erodes their ability to build or maintain a team.

These people tend to become stressed by heavy workloads. They do not like to delegate, and they do not prioritize tasks very well; as a result, they respond to increased workloads by working longer and harder—not smarter. Inevitably, quality begins to suffer, while they fall further and further behind, and they find this intolerable. At some point, their strengths turn into a weakness, and they become a bottleneck to productivity because everything must pass through them, be checked and revised by them, and be approved by them; they will not let anything go that is not completed according to their standards. As people move up in organizations, they must learn to delegate, prioritize, and decide what needs to be done well and what does not.

To work with these people, you must be prepared to be second guessed, to be closely supervised, and to be nagged. You can help by making suggestions regarding prioritizing work, and by putting tasks into context by reflecting on the big picture. At the same time, you can learn some lessons about work ethic and organizational citizenship.

Dutiful

Persons with high scores on this dimension are deeply concerned about being accepted, being liked, and getting along, especially with authority figures. They are alert for signs of disapproval, and equally alert for opportunities to ingratiate themselves, be of service, and demonstrate their fealty and loyalty to the organization. When they think they have given offense, they redouble their efforts to be model citizens. From the observer's perspective, what is most distinctive about these people is their good nature, their politeness, their cordiality, and their indecisiveness. They are very predictable, but as managers, they will do anything their boss requires; this means that they are reluctant to stick up for their staff or challenge authority, and this inevitably erodes their legitimacy as leaders.

At their best, these people are polite, conforming, and eager to please. Because they are so agreeable, they rarely make enemies. Because they seldom criticize anyone, complain about anything, or threaten anyone, they tend to rise in organizations. However, they have problems making decisions, taking initiative, or taking stands; consequently, the units for which they are responsible tend to drift, their staff feels unsupported, and they have trouble maintaining a team.

These people respond to stress and heavy workloads by freezing and becoming passive, and by hoping that someone else will take initiative, step up, make a decision, assign responsibility, and get things moving. Indeed, this usually happens; consequently, these people specialize in relying on the initiative of others. However, while they are waiting for someone else to take initiative, they become a bottleneck for productivity and a source of delay and lost time.

They are deeply concerned with pleasing authority, which is pleasing to authority, but they provide little leadership for those who must work for them. To work with these people, you must be prepared for indecisiveness, inaction, and lack of leadership. You must also be prepared to take initiative when processes get stalled, but accept the fact that you will not be supported should your initiative fail or backfire.

OTHER ISSUES

I have spent the past several years trying to demonstrate the importance of these derailing tendencies for managerial and executive careers, and to a large extent I have succeeded (cf. Dotlich & Cairo, 2003). However, there are other, less remarked on causes of managerial failure to which I allude only briefly. The most important of these causes fall into two broad categories. The first concerns the inability to get anything done, a point made earlier by Charan and Colvin (1999). Bruke and Ghosal (2002) interviewed more than 200 managers at Lufthansa in 2000 in an effort to find out what sort of things interfered with their ability to do their jobs. They then classified the various reasons why these managers were occupationally challenged, and arrayed them along two primary axes, called focus and energy. According to these researchers, the reasons that managers were unable to get anything done resulted from a lack of focus, a lack of energy, or both, and that is an exhaustive description of the causes.

What is most interesting in the article, and a fact on which the authors failed to comment, is that 90% of the managers in their sample were described as unable to get anything done. This raises an interesting question about the base rate of this particular challenge. If Bruke and Ghosal (2002) are taken seriously, then the base rate is 90%. In my view, this syndrome is a major problem among managers, a problem that is as important as it is not remarked on. My sense is that the typical exemplar of this problem is a person who is bright, charming, personable, and somewhat ditzy; because these people are so smart and engaging, others are willing to ignore their performance deficits. In any case, this represents an interesting area for future research.

The second important cause of managerial failure that psychologists have largely ignored is a character issue. It concerns bad values, specifically greed and selfishness. Greed and selfishness coexist with intelligence, drive, social skill, and charisma—all the characteristics on which assessment centers focus. Most of the recent high-profile cases of executive misbehavior—at Enron, Adelphi, Worldcom, Tyco, and so on—are instances of greed caused by bad values, not by flawed personalities. This is yet another interesting area for future research.

CONCLUSION

The popular press attests to the fact that bad management is rampant in the corporate world. Personal experience verifies the news from the popular press. Popular accounts of bad managers always turn into efforts to classify them into certain categories—the terms arrogant, insensitive, and self-centered come up over and over. This chapter argues that we now have a useful taxonomy of management derailment factors that is based in psychological theory and psychometric assessment, and we can define the major components of managerial incompetence.

TABLE 6.4
Strengths and Shortcomings of the Derailment Factors

Factor	Strengths	Shortcomings
1. Excitable	Empathy and concern	Emotional explosiveness
2. Skeptical	Social and political insight	Excessive suspicion
3. Cautious	Evaluates risks appropriately	Indecisiveness and risk aversion
4. Reserved	Emotionally unflappable	Insensitive and poor communicator
5. Leisurely	Good social skills	Passive aggression
6. Bold	Courage and energy	Overbearing and manipulative
7. Mischievous	Unafraid of risk	Reckless and deceitful
8. Colorful	Celebrations and entertainment	Impulsive and distractible
9. Imaginative	Creativity and vision	Bad ideas
10. Diligent	Hard work and high standards	Micromanagement
11. Dutiful	Corporate citizenship	Indecisiveness

I would like to propose a more nuanced view—namely, that there are strengths and weaknesses associated with the various derailment factors. Table 6.4 reviews these strengths and shortcomings. Every competent manager I have ever met has some elevation on dimensions 6 through 9 in Table 6.4; this seems to be where their energy, resilience, and ideas come from. Ultimately in human affairs, it comes down to *saphrosyne*, to balance, and to proportionality. Good things taken to the extreme turn into bad things.

7

How to Fix Incompetence

It isn't what you don't know that will hurt you, it's what you do know that isn't true.

—Will Rogers

This chapter makes the case that a very large percentage of managers and executives in the public and private spheres are underperforming, if not actually incompetent. This highlights the importance of helping managers develop their leadership skills. Executive coaching is one answer to this problem and has become a major growth industry that seems to be expanding even as the rest of the economy contracts. In addition to the issue of fixing leadership shortcomings, it is axiomatic in today's world of business that change is the only constant, and that successful managers must get on a learning treadmill just to keep up, but more important, to succeed.

A vast array of management training practices are available today, and it might be useful to define some landmarks to navigate the array. Despite the large number of training opportunities for managers today, there is no agreement on terminology, methods, or desired outcomes

(Peterson & Hicks, 1999). This chapter provides some definitions that should help map the conceptual landscape and some recommendations regarding the way forward.

The first question to ask is this: What, in the world of business and organizational behavior, changes and what does not change? What changes is technology, especially communications, data storage, retrieval, and transmission. The revolution in computing and telecommunications is in its early stages and is transforming every business from acupuncture to book selling. It has also transformed the world of finance, including capital markets and the governments in which they are located. These changes have come about quickly, they are permanent, and they reinforce the old rule: Adapt, migrate, or die. Consequently, changes in technology dictate that a lot of new learning must take place if managers are to remain credible among their peers.

It is also important to be clear about what does not change. The rapid shifts in technological capability in medicine, manufacturing, investing, and communications create the sense that all is flux, the feeling that we live in Democritus's universe of constant, swirling monadic chaos. The notion that everything is changing is further supported by those social theorists who argue that human nature is infinitely flexible and is shaped by the changing cultural, economic, and historical conditions that surround it. This view of human malleability is related to structural sociology, cultural anthropology, and situationist social psychology; it regards human nature as a work in progress, constantly reformed by sociohistorical forces (typically molded for the better, by the way; cf. Degler, 1991). One consequence of this assumption of infinite human malleability is the belief that organizations can and should be structured in any way that makes financial sense, regardless of the wishes of the staff and employees, who will be able to change and adapt to virtually any structure. In this model, the need to adapt creates more demand for continuous learning.

The problem is that this view of human malleability is wrong. There is a stable core to human nature; the stable core reflects the fact that humankind is a very old species and that people identical to us have been around for at least 100,000 years. Humans are, in fact, remarkably adaptable—adaptability is part of the stable core and one of the keys to our success as a species—and some people can modify certain components of their social behavior, including various skills and behaviors (Peterson, 1993). However, we are not infinitely adaptable. For example, our needs for love, companionship, status, and a sense of meaning and purpose in our lives are ancient and immutable desires. When these needs are frustrated for prolonged periods—by war, economic downturns, or just plain bad luck—people become demoralized, depressed, and dysfunctional. In short, although technology changes rapidly, human nature does not, and this fact has important implications for executive education. In my view, that which the newly minted military officer or MBA most needs to learn about is home truths about human nature. Professional education in business, engineering, and science (including, alas, psychology) largely concerns technical issues. Very little attention is ever given to a systematic analysis of human nature, including the needs, aspirations, and capabilities of the new junior manager. As a result, these people show up at work for the first time with a major gap in their intellectual toolkits, although they will normally believe, based on their past experience, that they know as much as is needed. This is the point of the Will Rogers quote with which this chapter began.

DEFINING LEARNING AND EDUCATION

What is learning? Education is the result of learning; a person who has learned a lot is said to be educated. We also distinguish degrees of education: A person who is well educated has not only learned a lot (which can be evaluated quantitatively), but has also learned the right things (which is more a matter of taste).

Psychologists define learning in two ways. The tradition of phenomenology and Gestalt psychology assumes that people construct mental models of the world, and then use the models to interpret reality and guide their behavior. Learning is equivalent to revising old or constructing new and enhanced mental models (Newell & Simon, 1972; Vosniadou & Brewer, 1987). Implicit in this tradition is the realization that mental models can be parochial, or even wrong (as Will Rogers quipped, "Good judgment is the result of experience, which is often the result of bad judgment"). Consider the Italian folktale *Pinocchio,* which Americans believe is a children's story; in fact, it is a cautionary tale for adults. Pinocchio is repeatedly duped by ruffians and this warns Italian peasants that city dwellers hold superior mental models that allow them to prey on their less sophisticated country cousins. For our purposes, one form of management education concerns shaping mental models—challenging unexamined assumptions and changing unconscious worldviews.

On the other hand, the tradition of behaviorism defines learning as a change in behavior after an experience. In this view, education involves acquiring or changing behaviors. People differ in terms of the number of behaviors they have available and their appropriateness. The concept of skill also comes in here: A skill is a particular kind of well-honed behavioral capacity. Defining learning in terms of skill acquisition suggests that the Gestalt and behaviorist models of learning concern very different phenomena. Thus, a person could have a profound understanding of the world but be unable to drive a car or balance a checkbook; conversely, a person could be an accomplished athlete, musician, or chess player but also be a bigot and a racist. In any case, a behaviorist model of learning would see management education as a process of acquiring skills, with no emphasis on the process of deeper understanding. Conversely, a Gestalt model of learning would see management education as a process of constructing mental models appropriate for interpreting organizational phenomenon, with no emphasis on the development of concrete skills. This is the same distinction that the British philosopher Ryle (1948) famously drew between the two forms of knowledge that he called knowing that and knowing how; *knowing that* refers to knowing that something is the case, whereas *knowing how* refers to knowing how to do something.

In principle, it makes sense to distinguish between the behaviorist and the Gestalt models of learning. In reality, however, the distinction may be arbitrary. There are two reasons for thinking so. First, research on skill acquisition has recognized for at least 20 years that mental rehearsal improves physical performance (cf. Heuer, 1985); this means that cognitive structures underlie and guide overt behavior and are therefore indistinguishable from behavior. More important, the Swiss developmental psychologist Piaget and the American educational psychologist Dewey had very similar notions about how we learn; their views can be summarized as, "Thought follows action," or "We learn by doing." In this pragmatist tradition, if we do something successfully, we then reflect on what we have done and create a mental model to guide our subsequent actions. Conversely and more important, if we do something and we fail, we normally set about trying to understand why we failed and what we should do next. Conceptual understanding (learning) follows action, but conceptual understanding (learning) depends on reflecting on the action. I find this perspective intellectually congenial; more important, it has the advantage of integrating the best insights of the behaviorist and the Gestalt traditions in a pragmatic marriage of convenience.

WHAT DRIVES LEARNING?

The behaviorist and Gestalt traditions also differ in terms of how they conceptualize the dynamics of learning. For the behaviorists, learning is driven by efforts to meet physiological needs (hunger, thirst, avoidance of pain) and shaped by the hedonic and instrumental consequences of these efforts. The mantra of the radical behaviorist Skinnerians is, "Behavior is a function of its consequences." More specifically, behaviors that are rewarded (that meet physiological needs) are learned, and behaviors that are not rewarded are not retained. This is the lesson of management primers such as *The One Minute Manager* and *Zap.* In this model, the acquisition of skills depends on rewards, not punishments.

In the Gestalt tradition, learning is driven by epistemic hunger, by a desire to understand or master the world—even at the expense of physiological needs. Learning is primarily shaped by errors and mistakes. For writers such as Jean Piaget, success carries limited information value; success means that we should continue doing what we have been doing. It is failure that challenges our understanding and drives us to reconceptualize the world. In this Gestalt view, we learn far more from our failures than our successes; the reorganization of mental models depends on failures, not rewards.

Learning and Development

Theories of learning are often tied to models of development and the links between the two depend on some unspecified assumptions. In the behaviorist tradition, development is essentially a random walk that varies across individuals and depends on the demands that come up during an individual life history. Specifically, development consists of learning new behaviors or skills as they become necessary in everyday life. The order in which the skills are developed depends on the order in which the problems come up in a person's life, which of course varies across lives. Timing is not necessarily important, so that earlier experiences are just earlier, not more influential. The direction of development is bidirectional and incremental—one can learn or unlearn skills as appropriate, and development consists of the steady layering of skills.

The classic developmental tradition, as exemplified by Freud, Erikson, and Piaget, views matters quite differently. Here development has a direction and an endpoint (from immaturity to maturity); development is internally programmed and spontaneously unfolds; it is stage-like and consists of qualitative transformations over time—persons at later stages of development are different qualitatively (they have different kinds of skills), not quantitatively (they have more skills). Finally, in classic developmental theory, early experiences are more important than later experiences. My point, however, is that these two developmental models have very different implications for executive learning. In the behaviorist tradition, learning new skills depends primarily on whether the necessary prior skills are available—so pretty much anything can be learned at any time. In the classic developmental tradition, however, the lessons (mental models) of adulthood can only be learned by adults; for example, Aristotle refused to teach ethics to anyone under the age of 30 because a degree of maturity was needed to understand the material. For Aristotle, it would be pointless to try to teach management skills to people who have never had any experience as managers. For the behaviorists, however, prior experience is not really necessary: If we teach new managers the relevant skills, transfer of training will take care of the rest.

The foregoing concerns theories of development, and the literature on the topic is fairly extensive. Surprisingly, however, the literature on the practice of development—on how to foster it—is undeveloped to the point of nonexistence. Hicks and Peterson (1999) presented an interesting model that describes the conditions necessary to bring about systematic personal development, and they provided a first step in the process of turning theory into practice.

Learning and Motivation

Models of learning are also tied to models of motivation. Academic discussions of motivation are hopelessly confused by a lack of clarity regarding the meaning of the key term. The word *motive* has two distinct meanings that need to be kept separate. On the one hand, motive refers to intentions; in management by objectives, for example, people who are committed to a program of action (i.e., who intend to follow it) are said to be motivated. On the other hand, motive refers to biological needs; for example, in Maslow's system, people are motivated by certain unmet needs, and the need that is important at any point in time depends on which of a set of five big ones have already been satisfied. These two definitions of motivation—motives as intentions and motives as biological drives—are essentially incommensurate. This makes it impossible to compare models of learning tied to different forms of motivation.

Many organizational psychologists adopt a model of motivation that is scientifically inadequate and is, therefore, a barrier to progress in understanding individual development. Specifically, many academics and practitioners have implicitly adopted Maslow's view that self-actualization is the most important human motive, and that training is most effective when it is linked to this growth motive. There are at least three reasons for rethinking this article of faith. First, according to Marx, self-actualization is the most important human motive; because of this, it is the responsibility of the state to provide the social conditions needed for its citizens to realize the powers that are latent within them. Maslow was a Marxist, he adopted this motivational assumption uncritically, and generations of management scientists have done the same. However, Marxism has been discredited on the world historical stage, and this casts some doubt on the validity of Marx's views of human nature. Second, although the concept of self-actualization has been an important part of modern psychology since the 1930s, as of today there are no well-validated measures of the concept. The reason there are no measures, I propose, is that there is nothing to measure—because the term does not refer to anything that actually exists. Finally, the concept of self-actualization makes no obvious sense from the perspective of evolutionary theory, which is the ultimate touchstone for all claims about human nature. A need for companionship makes evolutionary sense—companions can provide mutual aid—but what ends does self-actualization serve? Do self-actualized organisms have an adaptive advantage?

As noted in chapter 1, I believe there are three great metamotives in life. At a deep and often unconscious level, people need (a) acceptance and approval (and are stressed by rejection and criticism); (b) status, power, and the control of resources (and are stressed by their loss); and (c) predictability and order (and are stressed by their loss). People who lack social approval, power, and predictability in their lives are at serious risk for survival. These needs are biological, which means they are stable and enduring. It also means that there are individual differences in their urgency—some people need more social contact than others, some people need status more than others, some people need more predictability than others. It follows, based on these motivational assumptions, that the most consequential learning in life is organized around gaining acceptance and approval (or avoiding rejection); gaining status, power, and resource control (or minimizing their loss); and making sense out of the world. If learning can be tied to solving these problems—which are called getting along, getting ahead, and making sense—then the learning process assumes urgency, potency, and emotional significance.

A DOMAIN MODEL OF MANAGERIAL EDUCATION

In modern business parlance, the concept of skill has morphed into the concept of competence. As originally discussed by McClelland and his colleagues, a competency is a performance capability that distinguishes effective from ineffective managers in a particular organization (Boyatzis, 1982). McClelland defined competencies empirically, and they were specific to the requirements of a particular job in a particular context. This clear, specific, and rigorous definition has given way to ad hoc lists of organizational competencies defined by committees. Rather than criticize the confusions surrounding the modern enthusiasm for competencies, I simply note that all lists of competencies can be organized in terms of the domain model first proposed by Hogan and Warrenfeltz (2003). Table 7.1 provides an overview of the model.

Specifically, every current competency model can be described in terms of four competency domains; I refer to these competencies as:

TABLE 7.1

The Domain Model

Domain	Associated Competencies
Intrapersonal	Integrity and trust, patience, courage, self-discipline, self-confidence, perseverance, time management, composure, work ethic
Interpersonal	Approachability, customer focus, interpersonal savvy, listening, negotiations, peer relations, understanding others, communicating, compassion
Technical	Good decision making, drive for results, organizing, business acumen, process management, managing and measuring work, staying up to date
Leadership	Delegating, directing others, hiring and staffing, action orientation, motivating others, building effective teams, command skills, confronting poor performance, political savvy, ambition

(a) intrapersonal skills, (b) interpersonal skills, (c) leadership skills, and (d) business skills. I believe that these four domains define the content of management education. They also provide a basis for designing curricula, assigning people to training, and evaluating management education. Finally, these four domains form a natural, overlapping developmental sequence, with the later skills depending on the appropriate development of the earlier skills. They also form a hierarchy of trainability, with the earlier skills being hard to train and the later skills being easier to train.

Intrapersonal Skills

The domain of intrapersonal skills concerns characteristics that develop early—perhaps by age 5 or 6—and have important consequences for career development in adulthood. This domain seems to have four natural components. The first can be described as core self-esteem (Judge & Bono, 1999; Judge, Locke, Durham, & Kluger, 1998), emotional security, or perhaps resiliency. People with core self-esteem are self-confident; they have stable, positive moods; they are not easily frustrated or upset; and they bounce back quickly from reversals and disappointments. Persons who lack core self-esteem are self-critical, moody, unhappy, easily frustrated, hard to soothe, and need frequent reassurance and positive feedback. Core self-esteem is easy to measure, which means we can give managers reliable feedback on the subject. Moreover, measures of core self-esteem predict a wide variety of career outcomes, including job satisfaction and performance evaluations (Judge & Bono, 1999), which means clients should pay attention to feedback on this topic.

The second component of intrapersonal skills concerns attitudes toward authority. Persons with positive attitudes toward authority follow rules and respect procedures; they are compliant, conforming, socially appropriate, and easy to supervise. Persons with negative attitudes toward authority ignore rules and violate procedures; they are rebellious, refractory, and hard to supervise. Attitudes toward authority are easy to measure (Hogan & Hogan, 1989) and predict a wide variety of career outcomes, including supervisors' ratings of satisfactoriness. Thus, valid feedback on this topic can and should be incorporated in the learning process.

The third component of intrapersonal skills is self-control, the ability to restrain one's impulses, curb one's appetites, stay focused, maintain schedules, and follow routines. Persons with good self-control are self-disciplined, buttoned down, and abstemious. Persons with poor self-control are impulsive, self-indulgent, and undisciplined. Self-control is easy to measure and measures of self-control predict a wide variety of career outcomes (Hogan & Holland, 2003).

The fourth domain of intrapersonal skills concerns core values. Although skills and values are different concepts, we believe values belong in the intrapersonal domain for three reasons. First, they develop early in life, probably prior to age 10, so they develop contemporaneously with the other intrapersonal skills. Second, because values develop early, they tend to be unconscious, or at least to be part of the world taken for granted. This means that feedback about core values may be essential. Third, the fit between a person's core values and the corporate culture wherein he or she works is an important determinant of occupational performance.

Intrapersonal skill seems to be the core of the widely popular but scientifically suspect concept of EQ—scientifically suspect because the measurement base is so poorly developed. Intrapersonal skill is the foundation on which management careers are built. Persons with good intrapersonal skills project integrity; from the perspective of implicit leadership theory (i.e., what we expect to see in leaders), integrity is the first and perhaps the most important characteristic of leadership (Kouzes & Posner, 2002). Successful managers receive high scores on measures of intrapersonal skills, whereas highly effective salespeople and entrepreneurs receive low scores. This is one of the interesting and significant ways in which effective managers and sales personnel are different.

Interpersonal Skills

Interpersonal skills begin to develop after children leave the exclusive care of their parents and join the juvenile peer group—usually when they enter school around 5 or 6 years of age. People with interpersonal skills seem charming, poised, socially adept, approachable, and rewarding to deal with.

There are four components to interpersonal skills. The first is a disposition to put oneself in the place of another person, and try to anticipate what that person expects during an interaction. Mead (1934) referred to this as taking the role of the other. The second component is a skill and not a disposition; it involves getting it right when one tries to anticipate another person's expectations. This is the topic of accuracy in interpersonal perception (Funder, 2001), and it seems to be related to cognitive ability and social experience—bright extroverts are more accurate than dull introverts. The third component of interpersonal skill is a disposition; it involves incorporating the information about the other person's expectations into one's subsequent behavior. The final component of interpersonal skill involves having the self-control to stay focused on the other person's expectations; here interpersonal skill overlaps with intrapersonal skill.

Interpersonal skill concerns initiating, building, and maintaining relationships with a variety of people, some of whom might differ from oneself in terms of age, gender, ethnicity, social class, or political agendas. Interpersonal skill is easily measured, and good measures of interpersonal skill predict a wide range of occupational outcomes, including managerial performance (cf. Hogan & Hogan, 2001; Riggio, 1989). It is important to incorporate information about interpersonal skills into any training program.

Technical Skills

The domain of technical skills differs from the preceding two domains in several ways. It develops later, usually after a person enters the world of work, it is easier to train, it is mostly cognitive, and in an important way, it does not depend on being able to deal productively with others. Technical skills involve planning, monitoring budgets, forecasting costs and revenues, cutting costs, mapping strategies, evaluating performance, running meetings, and organizing necessary reports. For the most part, these activities can be performed in private and are easily modeled in an assessment center. They depend on cognitive ability rather than people skills, and they are the reason people believe cognitive ability is important for managerial performance. To the degree that organizations select and evaluate managers on the basis of cognitive ability and ignore interpersonal skill, they ignore the human side of enterprise.

Leadership Skills

The domain of leadership skills is perhaps the most extensively studied topic in management science (for a detailed review, see Hogan, Curphy, & Hogan, 1994; Hogan & Kaiser, 2005). I believe leadership skills can be understood in terms of five interrelated components that vitally depend on the availability of intrapersonal, interpersonal, and technical skills. Leadership skills are all about building and maintaining effective teams. The first component of leadership involves identifying the talent that a team actually needs and then persuading people with the right talent to join the team. The second component involves being able to retain talented personnel after they have been recruited—and simply throwing money at people is not sufficient. The third component of leadership skill concerns being able to motivate the team—other things being equal, a motivated team will outperform a more talented but less motivated group. Recruiting, retaining, and motivating team members depend on building positive relationships with each team member, a capability that builds on the interpersonal skills developed earlier. However, it also depends on having enough technical skill to be credible as a leader.

The fourth component of leadership skill concerns developing, projecting, and promoting a vision for the team. The vision legitimizes the team enterprise and the skills developed earlier will be needed to sell it. Projecting and promoting a vision is the essence of charisma; it is through the process of adopting a vision that people are able to transcend their selfish interests and develop what Durkheim (1925) called impersonal ends for their actions. Durkheim also considered developing impersonal ends for one's actions to be an essential feature of moral conduct; it is only in this way that people can overcome their innate selfishness.

The final component of leadership skill concerns wanting to win, to prevail, to make an impact or a difference, to create a legacy, and to outperform the other teams with which one competes. The desire to win seems related to the core values that develop early.

THE INNER–OUTER DISTINCTION

As noted in chapter 1, it is important to distinguish two perspectives on a person's performance; I referred to these as the inner and the outer perspective, or as the perspective of the actor and the perspective of the observer. The inner perspective concerns a person's self-view, his or her goals and aspirations, and self-evaluations of current skills and past performance. This is what we mean by a person's identity. The outer perspective concerns how a person's performance is evaluated by others. It concerns other people's views of a person's skills, accomplishments, and future potential. This is what we mean by a person's reputation. The domain model we have just presented is best defined in terms of ratings provided by other people rather than by individuals themselves.

The inner and outer perspectives are unique and distinct. Although most of us are largely preoccupied with the first—with our own self-evaluations—the second—others' evaluations of our performance—is substantially more consequential in terms of real world payoff. For example, self-ratings of leadership performance are poorly correlated with actual leadership performance (Hogan et al., Hogan, 1994), although some people are better at making these self-appraisals accurately than others. What people have to say about themselves is largely a theory about their own performance; it is a theory that is rarely tested or evaluated, and in some cases it is shockingly out of touch with reality. In short, self-evaluations of performance capabilities and successes are not very reliable data sources.

On the other hand, other people's evaluations are important sources of information. These evaluations are reliable, in the sense that if properly collected, they will converge. They are relatively easy to obtain. They are related to occupational performance—indeed, other people's evaluations are, in a real sense, the same as occupational performance. Performance appraisals always reflect the views of others; bosses' evaluations are the primary key to salary increases and promotions.

The distinction between self-knowledge (what we believe to be the case about us) and other knowledge (what others believe to be the case about us) is a key consideration for executive education. In terms of the domain model, it is a matter of some importance to know how others evaluate your intrapersonal skills. Although we do not believe that a person's self-control, moodiness, and attitudes toward authority can be educated in a profound way, a person can be made aware of the fact that others perceive him or her as, for example, impulsive, insubordinate, and bad tempered. Then he or she can construct strategies for dealing with the negative consequences of poor intrapersonal skills. In the absence of such feedback information, however, a person will tend to be a victim of his or her childhood (cf. Kaplan & Kaiser, 2001).

In the same way, people are typically poor judges of their own interpersonal skills. Again, feedback from others will be more informative than introspection, and this feedback is a core component of executive education. Although interpersonal skills are hard to coach, they are more malleable than intrapersonal skills, and with the proper feedback, time, and attention, people can become more approachable, responsive, and attentive, and can learn to at least seem to feel another person's pain.

As for leadership skills, other people in general, and subordinates in particular, are the best single source of information regarding a person's performance as a leader. In our experience, people are poor judges of their own performance as leaders, and this view is supported by considerable data (cf. Hogan et al., 1994).

As for technical skills, because they have such a heavy cognitive loading, the inner–outer distinction is less important. People are able to evaluate their business skills pretty well. However, I would emphasize that, in the absence of reasonable leadership skills, good technical skills will not really matter.

INDIVIDUAL DIFFERENCES

People respond differently to the same educational experiences, and the differences in their responses are predictable and interpretable, not randomly distributed.

This section points out where the areas of resistance to education will lie. More specifically, it describes the characteristics of executives that will make education difficult for them. I believe that four individual difference variables affect executive learning and they are as follows.

1. Individual differences in self-control will affect a person's learning style in the following way. People who are self-disciplined can focus for extended periods, stay on task, concentrate on details, and generally make conscientious students who are well liked by teachers and coaches. Conversely, impulsive people are easily bored and distracted, have short attention spans, dislike details, and generally are indifferent students, unless they really care about the subject matter. Once again, self-control is easy to measure, and good measures of self-control predict academic performance above and beyond cognitive ability (Ones, Viswesvaran, & Schmidt, 1993). Self-control is part of what I referred to earlier as intrapersonal skills.

2. Individual differences in self-confidence influence learning in an interesting and counterintuitive manner. Persons who are highly self-confident resist coaching and feedback—because they are generally hard to influence. Self-confident people are particularly resistant to bad news, criticism, and negative feedback. On the one hand, this makes them resilient and able to bounce back quickly from rever-

sals—because they do not perceive themselves has having made mistakes or possibly failed. On the other hand, because they have trouble acknowledging their mistakes, they are unable to learn from them. The optimal way to coach such people is by focusing on the positive and trying to shape their behavior in a Skinnerian way; behaviorism works because such people will only listen to positive feedback.

People with low self-confidence are also hard to coach because they are on the alert for anything that sounds like criticism, and become defensive when they hear it. Because of their defensiveness, they have trouble testing their ideas about how others perceive them. Because they avoid negative feedback, they have a great deal of trouble reorganizing their mental models. The best way to coach such people is to remind them constantly of their strengths, and encourage them to embrace as much reality as they can tolerate.

Curiously, it is the people with average self-confidence who are the easiest to coach. They are self-critical and willing to believe negative feedback, but they have enough self-confidence to be willing to try new ways of thinking and behaving. They will listen to criticism and feedback, and internalize it. Self-confidence is also part of what I referred to earlier as intrapersonal skills.

3. People differ quite substantially in terms of how insightful they are about other people. Individual differences in perceptiveness are easily measured (cf. Hogan & Hogan, 2001), they are modestly related to cognitive ability, and perceptiveness is part of the domain referred to earlier as interpersonal skills. Perceptive people can quickly and intuitively understand what motivates others, and they tend to avoid management practices that gratuitously upset and alienate their staff. They also understand the point of discussions about motivation and morale. People who are less perceptive are basically indifferent to the feelings and expectations of others, and tend to prefer influence tactics based on power rather than finesse. They will think about motivation in terms of money and self-interest, advocate a hard-nosed version of capitalism, and regard concern for morale and staff expectations to be rank sentimentality (cf. Zaccaro, 2002).

4. People also differ in terms of their rationality (Stanovich, 1999); some people prefer to base their opinions, judgments, and decisions on data, and are willing to use data to evaluate the consequences of their decisions. Other people prefer to operate in a more intuitive manner, and base their opinions and decisions on experi-

ence and "gut instinct." In addition, they tend to be uninterested in evaluating their decisions and are reluctant to change their opinions when they have been disconfirmed (Epstein, Pacini, Denes-Raj, & Heier, 1996). Individual differences in rationality will influence both the methods for, and the success of, executive education. Individual differences in rationality are easy to measure, and measures of rationality predict performance in problem-solving tasks over and above measures of cognitive ability. To the degree that learning is defined as a change in mental models, individual differences in rationality will influence the way executives process educational material. Those who base their views on data will want to see more empirically based arguments, whereas those who prefer to make intuitive decisions will respond better to anecdotes, hortatory messages, and examples involving single cases.

OUTCOMES

Although corporations spend billions of dollars each year on training, experts report that training interventions are rarely evaluated in terms of the degree to which they achieve their professed goals, or in terms of their influence on the bottom line. The same is true for executive coaching and education, which are specialized training interventions for elite groups; I am unaware of any systematic evaluations of coaching programs (cf. Burke & Day, 1986; Kaiser & DeVries, 2000). Given the explosive growth in coaching programs (and the fact that I prefer rational arguments), what kind of case can be made for the effectiveness of coaching?

Clinical psychologists have been concerned for years with evaluating the effects of their training interventions; the insurance companies that pay for the interventions gave added impetus to this concern. We think outcome research in clinical psychology is a reasonable place to look for evidence regarding the effectiveness of executive coaching for four reasons. First, psychotherapy is quite intensive, one-on-one coaching. Although it is organized around a search for the source of an individual's problems, it bears at least a family resemblance to coaching, which usually concerns determining the kinds of mistakes an executive typically makes. Second, executives often begin coaching because they are having problems getting along in their organizations. Although few of them are neurotic, many of them are overly aggressive, narcissistic, histrionic, or just plain mean, and the coaching involves dealing with these interpersonal flaws. Third, much of what goes on under the rubric of executive coaching is in essence psychotherapy. The goal is not to improve the person's leadership skills but to make the person feel better about himself or herself. Finally, some data are better than no data (rationality, again), and there are some interesting data regarding the effectiveness of psychotherapy.

The literature evaluating the effectiveness of psychotherapy since World War II can be summarized in terms of two major generalizations. Glossing over the usual academic qualifications, people who undergo psychotherapy get better faster than people who do not, independent of the type of therapy, the length of therapy, the nature of the original problem, or the form of the outcome evaluation (Smith, Glass, & Miller, 1980). This suggests that executives who undergo coaching will also improve their performance more quickly than those who do not. This is true in part because the processes in therapy and coaching are so similar, but also because the key to successful therapy is that the client must want to change. Executives, as a group, are competitive people who are looking for any edge over their rivals, and most of them will take coaching very seriously indeed.

The second generalization is that therapy works more efficiently if it is preceded by an assessment (Fischer, 1994). Finn (1996) recommended asking clients what they want to learn from assessment feedback; at that time he also takes an objective measure of the clients' perceived ability to deal with their problems. He then does a psychological assessment and, in the second session, uses the feedback results to answer the clients' original questions. After the session, he retakes a measure of his clients' perceived ability to deal with their problems. Finn reported finding as much measured improvement in his clients after 2 sessions as other therapists get after 10 sessions of standard talk therapy. In my view, every training intervention should begin with an assessment, because if you do not know where you are going, any road will get you there.

In perhaps the most important study to date evaluating the effects of coaching, Peterson (1993) followed 370 executives between 1987 and 1992. These people went through a detailed assessment, received feedback, and then underwent 6 months of coaching (1 day per month), for a total of 50 hours. Each person received individualized coaching around specific objectives. Ratings on progress by the coach, the executive, and the executive's boss were collected at three points in time, and the results indicated most of the participants' performance as leaders improved as a result of the coaching experience.

SUMMARY

In this chapter, I tried to make six points as follows. First, learning outcomes fall into two broad categories. People can learn skills, and they can learn ways of conceptualizing reality—knowing how and knowing that.

Second, education should be organized around the most important human motives, and these motives concern learning how to get along with others, to get ahead in one's career, and to make sense out of one's life.

Third, the content of executive education can be organized in terms of a domain model with four components: intrapersonal skills, interpersonal skills, technical skills, and leadership skills.

Fourth, executive coaching should begin with an assessment of a person's standing in the four domains of executive skill. Feedback on the assessment should try to make a person aware of how others evaluate him or her in terms of the four domains of executive skill, and designing a program to change the evaluations that come up short.

Fifth, executive coaching organized in this way will probably work; in any case, change will occur much more rapidly than simply talking about a person's strengths and shortcomings.

Finally, education designed to allow managers to stay up to date on changes in technology falls under the category of training business skills, the third component of our domain model of competency development. Here the training process should be aligned with the individual's learning style.

References

Allport, G. W. (1954). The historical background of modern social psychology. In G. Lindzey (Ed.), *Handbook of social psychology* (vol. I, pp. 3–56). Cambridge, MA: Addison-Wesley.

Anderson, J. R., & Terrell, M. E. (2004). Too good to be true: CEOs and financial reporting fraud. *Consulting Psychology Journal, 56*(1), 35–43.

Antonakis, J., & Atwater, L. (2002). Leader distance: A review and a proposed theory. *Leadership Quarterly, 13,* 673–704.

Austin, J. R., & Bartunek, J. M. (2003). Theories and practices of organizational development. In W. C. Borman, D. R. Ilgen, & R. J. Klimoski (Eds.), *Handbook of psychology* (Vol. 12, pp. 309–332). New York: Wiley.

Avolio, B. J., Sosik, J. J., Jung, D. I., & Berson, Y. (2003). Leadership models, methods, and applications. In W. C. Borman, D. R. Ilgen, & R. J. Klimoski (Eds.), *Handbook of psychology* (Vol 12, pp. 277–301). Hoboken, NJ: Wiley.

Bandura, A. (1963). *Social learning and personality development.* New York: Free Press.

Barrett, L., Dunbar, R., & Lycett, J. (2002). *Human evolutionary psychology.* London: Palgrave.

Barrick, M. R., Day, D. V., Lord, R. G., & Alexander, R. A. (1991). Assessing the utility of executive leadership. *Leadership Quarterly, 2,* 9–22.

Barrick, M. R., Stewart, G. L., Neubert, M. J., & Mount, M. K. (1998). Relating member ability and personality to work-team processes and team effectiveness. *Journal of Applied Psychology, 83,* 377–391.

Barron, F. (1965). The psychology of creativity. In *New directions in psychology II* (pp. 1–120). New York: Holt, Rinehart, & Winston.

Bass, B. M. (1990). *Bass and Stogdill's handbook of leadership: Theory, research, and managerial applications* (3rd ed.). New York: Free Press.

Belbin, R. M. (1981). *Management teams: Why they succeed or fail.* London: Heineman.

Bentz, V. J. (1967). The Sears experience in the investigation, description, and prediction of executive behavior. In F. Wickert & D. E. McFarland (Eds.), *Measuring executive effectiveness* (pp. 147–206). New York: Appleton-Century-Crofts.

Bentz, V. J. (1990). Contextual issues in predicting high-level leadership performance. In K. E. Clark, & M. B. Clark (Eds.), *Measures of leadership* (pp. 131–144). West Orange, NJ: Leadership Library of America.

Bernreuter, R. G. (1933). The theory and construction of the personality inventory. *Journal of Social Psychology, 4,* 387–405.

Boehm, C. (1999). *Hierarchy in the forest.* Cambridge, MA: Harvard University Press.

Bourdieu, P. (1984). *Distinction: A social critique of the judgment of taste.* Cambridge, MA: Harvard University Press.

Bowlby, J. (1969). *Attachment and loss* (Vol. I). New York: Basic Books.

Boyatzis, R. A. (1982). *The competent manager.* New York: Wiley.

Browne, J. (2002). *Charles Darwin: The power of place.* New York: Knopf.

Bruke, H., & Ghosal, S. (2002, February). Beware the busy manager. *Harvard Business Review,* pp. 62–69.

Buchanan, J. M. (1977). *Freedom in constitutional contract: Perspective of a political economist.* College Station: Texas A&M Press.

Burke, M. J., & Day, R. R. (1986). A cumulative study of the effectiveness of managerial training. *Journal of Applied Psychology, 71,* 232–246.

Buss, A. H. (1997). Evolutionary perspectives on personality traits. In R. Hogan, J. Johnson, & S. Briggs (Eds.), *Handbook of personality psychology* (pp. 345–366). San Diego, CA: Academic.

Butcher, J. N., Dahlstrom, W. G., Graham, J. R., Tellegen, A., & Kaemmer, B. (1989). *Multiphasic Personality Inventory (MMPI-2): Manual for administration and scoring.* Minneapolis: University of Minnesota Press.

Cascio, W. (1998). *Applied psychology in human resource management* (5th ed.). Upper Saddle River, NJ: Prentice Hall.

Charan, R., & Colvin, G. (1999, June 21). Why CEO's fail. *Fortune,* 69–82.

Cherns, A. (1976). The principles of sociotechnical design. *Human Relations, 29,* 783–792.

Collins, J. (2002). *Good to great.* New York: HarperCollins.

Costa, P. T., Jr., & McCrae, R. R. (1988). Personality in adulthood: A six-year longitudinal study of self-reports and spouse ratings on the NEO Personality Inventory. *Journal of Personality and Social Psychology, 54,* 853–863.

Curphy, G. (2004). *High performance teams.* St. Paul, MN: Curphy Consulting Group.

Cyert, R., & Marsh, J. (1963). *A behavioral theory of the firm.* Englewood Cliffs, NJ: Prentice Hall.

Dawkins, R. (1976). *The selfish gene.* Oxford: Oxford University Press.

Day, D. V., & Lord, R. G. (1988). Executive leadership and organizational performance. *Journal of Management, 14,* 453–464.

Degler, C. N. (1991). *In search of human nature: The decline and revival of Darwinism in American social thought.* New York: Oxford University Press.

DeHartog, L. (2000). *Genghis Khan: Conqueror of the world.* London: Tauris Academic Studies.

Deming, W. E. (1986). *Out of crisis.* Cambridge, MA: Massachusetts Institute of Technology, Center for Advanced Engineering Study.

Diamond, J. (1997). *Guns, germs, and steel.* London: Vintage.

Dirks, K. T., & Ferrin, D. L. (2002). Trust in leadership: Meta-analytic findings and implications for research and practice. *Journal of Applied Psychology, 87,* 611–628.

Dixon, N. (1991). *On the psychology of military incompetence.* New York: Time Warner.

Dotlich, D. L., & Cairo, P. C. (2003). *Why CEOs fail.* San Francisco: Jossey-Bass.

Driskell, J. E., Hogan, R., & Salas, E. (1987). Personality and group performance. In C. Hendrick (Ed.), *Personality and social psychology review* (pp. 92–112). Palo Alto, CA: Sage.

Dulewicz, V. (1995). A validation of Belbin's team roles from 16PF and OPQ using bosses' ratings of competence. *Journal of Occupational and Organizational Psychology, 68,* 1–18.

Durkheim, E. (1925). *L'Education morale* [Moral Education]. Paris: Librairie Felix Alcan.

Emler, N. P. (2003, June). *Why the moral credentials of leaders matter.* Paper presented at the New Directions in Leadership Research conference sponsored by the European Association of Experimental Social Psychology, Amsterdam.

Epstein, S., Pacini, R, Denes-Raj, V., & Heier, H. (1996). Individual differences in intuitive-experiential and analytical-rational thinking styles. *Journal of Personality and Social Psychology, 71,* 390–405.

Fernandez-Araoz, C. (1999, July–August). Hiring without firing. *Harvard Business Review,* pp. 109–120.

Fiedler, F. E. (1967). *A theory of leadership effectiveness.* New York: McGraw-Hill.

Finn, S. E. (1996). *Manual for using the MMPI–2 as a therapeutic intervention.* Minneapolis: University of Minnesota Press.

Fischer, C. T. (1994). *Individualizing psychological assessment.* Hillsdale, NJ: Lawrence Erlbaum Associates.

Fleishman, E. A. (1989). *Examiner's manual for the Supervisor Behavior Description Questionnaire* (rev. ed.). Chicago: Science Research Associates.

Flynn, J. R. (1999). Searching for justice: The discovery of IQ gains over time. *American Psychologist, 54,* 5–20.

French, J. R. P., & Raven, B. H. (1959). The bases of social power. In D. Cartwright (Ed.), *Studies in social power* (pp. 150–167). Ann Arbor: University of Michigan Press.

Frenz, H. (Ed.). (1969). *Nobel lectures, literature 1901–1967.* Amsterdam: Elsevier.

Funder, D. C. (1987). Errors and mistakes: Evaluating the accuracy of social judgment. *Psychological Bulletin, 101,* 75–90.

Funder, D. C. (2001). Accuracy in personality judgment. In B. W. Roberts & R. Hogan (Eds.), *Personality psychology in the workplace* (pp. 121–140). Washington, DC: American Psychological Association.

Ghiselli, E. E., & Barthol, R. P. (1953). The validity of personality inventories in the selection of employees. *Journal of Applied Psychology, 37,* 18–20.

Goffman, E. (1959). *The presentation of self in everyday life.* Garden City, NY: Anchor.

Goleman, D. (1995). *Emotional intelligence: Why it can matter more than IQ.* New York: Bantam.

Golembiewski, R. T. (1962). *The small group.* Chicago: University of Chicago Press.

Gottlieb, G. (2000). Environmental and behavioral influences on gene activity. *Current Directions in Psychological Science, 9,* 93–97.

Gough, H. G. (1954). *Manual for the California Psychological Inventory.* Palo Alto, CA: Consulting Psychologists Press.

Guilford, J. P., Christiansen, P. R., Bond, N. A., & Sutton, M. A. (1954). A factor analysis study of human interests. *Psychological Monographs, 68*(Whole No. 375).

Guion, R. M., & Gottier, R. F. (1965). Validity of personality measures in personnel selection. *Personnel Psychology, 18,* 135–164.

Hackman, J. R., & Morris, C. G. (1975). Group tasks, group interaction process, and group performance effectiveness. In L. Berkowitz (Ed.), *Advances in experimental social psychology* (Vol. 8, pp. 45–99). New York: Academic.

Hackman, J. R., & Oldham, G. R. (1976). Motivation through the design of work. *Organizational Behavior and Human Performance, 16,* 250–279.

Hambrick, D. C. (1994). Top management groups. *Research in Organizational Behavior, 16,* 171–213.

Harter, J. K., Schmidt, F. L., & Hayes, T. L. (2002). Business-unit-level relationship between employee satisfaction, employee engagement, and business outcomes: A meta-analysis. *Journal of Applied Psychology, 87,* 268–279.

Haythorn, W. W. (1968). The composition of groups: A review of the literature. *Acta Psychologica, 28,* 97–128.

Herzberg, F. (1966). *Work and the nature of man.* Cleveland, OH: World Book.

Heuer, H. (1985). Wie wirkt mentale Ubung? [We use mental structures?]. *Psycholgische Rundschau, 36,* 191–200.

Hicks, M. D., & Peterson, D. B. (1999). The development pipeline: How people really learn. *Knowledge Management Review, 9,* 30–33.

Hirschey, M., & Wichern, D. (1984). Accounting and market-value measures of profitability. *Journal of Business Economics and Statistics, 2,* 375–383.

Hogan, R. (1973). Moral conduct and moral character. *Psychological Bulletin, 79,* 217–232.

Hogan, R. (1975). Theoretical egocentrism and the problem of compliance. *American Psychologist, 30,* 533–540.

Hogan, R. (1982). A socioanalytic theory of personality. In M. Page & R. Dienstbier (Eds.), *Nebraska symposium on motivation.* Lincoln: University of Nebraska Press.

Hogan, R. (2004). Personality psychology for organizational researchers. In B. Schneider & D. B. Smith (Eds.), *Personality and organizations* (pp. 3–24). Mahwah, NJ: Lawrence Erlbaum Associates.

Hogan, R. (2005). In defense of personality measurement: New wine for old whiners. *Human Performance, 18,* 331–341.

Hogan, R., Curphy, G., & Hogan, J. (1994). What we know about leadership: Effectiveness and personality. *American Psychologist, 51,* 469–477.

Hogan, R., Curphy, G., & Hogan, J. (1994). What we know about leadership. *American Psychologist, 49,* 493–504.

Hogan, R., Driskell, J. E., & Raza, S. (1988). Personality, team performance, and organizational context. In P. Whitney & R. B. Ochsman (Eds.), *Psychology and productivity* (pp. 93–103). New York: Plenum.

Hogan, R., & Henley, N. (1969). Nomotics: Toward a science of human rule systems. In *Proceedings of the 77th annual convention of the American Psychological Association* (pp. 443–444).

Hogan, R., & Hogan, J. (1989). How to measure employee reliability. *Journal of Applied Psychology, 74,* 273–279.

Hogan, R., & Hogan, J. (1991). Personality and status. In D. G. Gilbert & J. J. Conley (Eds.), *Personality, social skills, and psychopathology* (pp. 137–154). New York: Plenum.

Hogan, R., & Hogan, J. (1995). *Hogan Personality Inventory manual* (2nd ed.). Tulsa, OK: Hogan Assessment Systems.

Hogan, R., & Hogan, J. (1996). *Motives, Values, Preferences Inventory manual.* Tulsa, OK: Hogan Assessment Systems.

Hogan, R., & Hogan, J. (1997). *Manual for the Hogan Development Survey.* Tulsa, OK: Hogan Assessment Systems.

Hogan, R., & Hogan, J. (2001). Assessing leadership: A view from the dark side. *International Journal of Selection and Assessment, 9,* 1–12.

Hogan, R., & Hogan, J. (2002). The Hogan Personality Inventory. In B. de Raad & M. Perugini (Eds.), *Big Five assessment* (pp. 329–352). Gottingen, Germany: Hogrefe & Huber.

Hogan, J., & Holland, B. (2003). Using theory to evaluate personality and job performance relations: A socioanalytic perspective. *Journal of Applied Psychology, 88,* 100–112.

Hogan, R., & Kaiser, R. B. (2005). What we know about leadership. *Review of General Psychology, 9,* 169–180.

Hogan, R., & Roberts, B. (2000). A socioanalytic perspective on person/environment interaction. In W. B. Walsh, K. H. Craik, & R. H. Price (Eds.), *New directions in person–environment psychology* (pp. 1–24). Mahwah, NJ: Lawrence Erlbaum Associate.

Hogan, R., & Stokes, L. W. (2006). Business susceptibility to consulting fads: The case of emotional intelligence. In K. R. Murphy (Ed.), *A critique of emotional intelligence* (pp. 263–280). Mahwah, NJ: Lawrence Erlbaum Associates.

Hogan, R., & Warrenfeltz, R. W. (2003). Educating the modern manager. *Academy of Management Learning and Education, 2,* 74–84.

Hogg, M. A. (2001). A social identity theory of leadership. *Personality and Social Psychology Review, 5,* 184–200.

Holland, J. L. (1986). *Making vocational choices* (2nd ed.). Englewood Cliffs, NJ: Prentice Hall.

Holland, J. L. (1997). *Making vocational choices: A theory of vocational personalities and work environments* (3rd ed). Odessa, FL: PAR.

Hunt, J. G. (1991). *Leadership: A new synthesis.* Newbury Park, CA: Sage.

Jensen, A. (1969). How much can we boost IQ in scholastic achievement? *Harvard Educational Review, 39,* 1–123.

Joyce, W. F., Nohria, N., & Roberson, B. (2003). *What really works: The 4+2 formula for sustained business success.* New York: Harper Business.

Judge, T. A., & Bono, J. E. (1999, April). *Core self-evaluation and construct breadth.* Paper presented at the 14th annual conference of the Society of Industrial and Organizational Psychology, Atlanta, GA.

Judge, T. A., Bono, J. E., Ilies, R., & Gerhardt, M. W. (2002). Personality and leadership. *Journal of Applied Psychology, 87,* 765–780.

Judge, T., Erez, A., & Bono, J. E. (1998). The power of being positive: The relationship between positive self-concept and job performance. *Human Performance, 11,* 167–178.

Judge, T. A., Locke, E. A., Durham, D. D., & Kluger, A. N. (1998). Dispositional effects on job and life satisfaction: The role of core evaluations. *Journal of Applied Psychology, 83,* 17–34.

Kaemmer, B. (1989). *Minnesota Multiphasic Personality Inventory (MMPI–2): Manual for administration and scoring.* Minneapolis: University of Minnesota Press.

Kahan, J. P., Webb, N., Shavelson, R. J., & Stolzenberg, R. M. (1985). *Individual characteristics and unit performance.* Santa Monica, CA: Rand.

Kaiser, R. B., & DeVries, D. L. (2000). Leadership training. In W. E. Craighead & C. B. Nemeroff (Eds.), *The Corsini encyclopedia of psychology and behavioral science* (3rd ed.). New York: Wiley.

Kaplan, R. E., & Kaiser, R. B. (2001). *How sensitivities throw off performance in executives.* Greensboro, NC: Center for Creative Leadership.

Kaplan, R. E., & Kaiser, R. B. (2003a, June–July). Developing versatile leadership. *MIT Sloan Management Review, 4*(4), 19–26.

Kaplan, R. E., & Kaiser, R. B. (2003b). Rethinking a classic distinction in leadership. *Consulting Psychology Journal, 85,* 15–25.

Katz, D., & Kahn, R. L. (1978). *The social psychology of organizations.* New York: Wiley.

Kellerman, B. (2004, January). Leadership—Warts and all. *Harvard Business Review*, 40–45.

Kenrick, D. T., & Funder, D. C. (1988). Profiting from controversy: Lessons from the person–situation debate. *American Psychologist, 43,* 23–34.

Klimoski, R. J., & Mohammed, S. (1994). Team mental model: Construct or metaphor? *Journal of Management, 20,* 403–437.

Kornhauser, A. (1930). The study of work feelings. *Personnel Journal, 8,* 348–351.

Koslowski, S. W. J., & Bell, B. S. (2003). Work groups and teams in organizations. In W. C. Borman, D. R. Ilgen, & R. J. Klimoski (Eds.), *Handbook of psychology* (Vol. 12, pp. 333–376). New York: Wiley.

Kouzes, J. M., & Posner, B. Z. (2002). *The leadership challenge* (3rd ed.). San Francisco: Jossey-Bass.

Lawler, E. E., III, Mohrman, S. A., & Ledford, G. E., Jr. (1992). *Employee involvement and total quality management.* San Francisco: Jossey-Bass.

Leonard, H. S. (2003). Leadership development for the postindustrial, postmodern information age. *Consulting Psychology Journal, 55,* 3–14.

LePine, J. A., Hollenbeck, J. R., Ilgen, D. R., & Hedlund, J. (1997). Effects of individual differences on the performance of hierarchical decision-making teams. *Journal of Applied Psychology, 82,* 803–811.

Levine, J. M., & Moreland, R. L. (1990). Progress in small group research. *Annual Review of Psychology, 41,* 585–634.

Lombardo, M. M., Ruderman, M. N., & McCauley, C. D. (1987, August). *Explorations of success and derailment in upper level management positions.* Paper presented at meeting of the Academy of Management, New York.

Lord, R. G., DeVader, C. L., & Alliger, G. (1986). A meta-analysis of the relation between personality traits and leader perceptions. *Journal of Applied Psychology, 71,* 402–410.

Lord, R. G., Foti, R. J., & DeVader, C. L. (1984). A test of leadership categorization theory. *Organizational Behavior and Human Performance, 34,* 343–378.

MacIntyre, A. C. (1958). *The unconscious.* London: Routledge & Kegan Paul.

Mann, R. D. (1959). A review of the relationship between personality and performance in small groups. *Psychological Bulletin, 56,* 241–270.

March, J. G., & Olsen, J. (1976). *Ambiguity and choice in organizations.* Bergen, Norway: Universitetsforlaget.

March, J. G., & Olsen, J. (1982). The new institutionalism: Organizational factors in political life. *American Political Science Review, 78,* 734–749.

March, J. G., & Simon, H. A. (1958). *Organizations.* New York: Wiley.

Maynard-Smith, J. (1982). *Evolution and the theory of games.* Cambridge, UK: Cambridge University Press.

McAdams, D. (1993). *The stories we live by: Personal myths and the making of the self.* New York: Morrow.

McCall, M. W., Jr. , & Lombardo, M. M. (1983). *Off the track: Why and how successful executives get derailed* (Tech. Rep. No. 21). Greensboro, NC: Center for Creative Leadership.

McCormick, E. J., Finn, R. H., & Scheirs, D. C. (1957). Patterns of job requirements. *Journal of Applied Psychology, 41,* 358–364.

McCrae, R. R., & Costa, P. T., Jr. (1997). Personality trait structure as a human universal. *American Psychologist, 52,* 509–516.

McGrath, J. E. (1984). *Groups: Interaction and performance.* Englewood Cliffs, NJ: Prentice Hall.

Mead, G. H. (1934). *Mind, self, and society.* Chicago: University of Chicago Press.

Milgram, S. (1963). Behavioral study of obedience. *Journal of Abnormal and Social Psychology, 67,* 371–378.

Miller, D., Kets de Vries, M. F. R., & Toulouse, J.-M. (1982). Top executive locus of control and its relationship to strategy-making, structure, and environment. *Academy of Management Journal, 25,* 237–253.

Mintzberg, H. (1973). *The nature of managerial work.* New York: Harper & Row.

ischel, W. (1968). *Personality and assessment.* New York: Wiley.

Morris, C. G. (1966). Task effects on group interaction. *Journal of Personality and Social Psychology, 5,* 545–554.

Mumford, M. D. (Ed.). (2004). Leading for innovation: Part 2: Macro studies [Special issue]. *The Leadership Quarterly, 15* (Whole No. 1).

Myers, I. B., & McCauley, M. H. (1985). *Manual: A guide to the development and use of the Myers–Briggs Type Indicator.* Palo Alto, CA: Consulting Psychologists Press.

Neuman, G. A., & Wright, J. (1999). Team effectiveness: Beyond skills and cognitive ability. *Journal of Applied Psychology, 84,* 376–389.

Newell, A., & Simon, H. A. (1972). *Human problem solving.* Englewood Cliffs, NJ: Prentice Hall.

Nicholson, N. (2000). *Managing the human animal.* New York: Thomson.

Ones, D. S., Viswesvaran, C., & Schmidt, F. L. (1993). Comprehensive meta-analysis of integrity test validities: Findings and implications for personnel selection and theories of job performance [Monograph]. *Journal of Applied Psychology, 78,* 679–703.

O'Reilly, C. A., III, Chatman, J., & Caldwell, D. F. (1991). People and organizational culture: A profile comparison approach to assessing person–organizational fit. *Academy of Management Journal, 34,* 487–516.

Out of step with the Army. (2000, April 24). *Washington Post,* p. 3.

Paul, A. M. (2004). *The cult of personality.* New York: Free Press.

Peterson, D. B. (1993, April). *Measuring change: A psychometric approach to evaluating individual coaching outcomes.* Paper presented at the annual conference of the Society for Industrial and Organizational Psychology, San Francisco.

Peterson, D. B., & Hicks, M. D. (1999, May). *The art and practice of executive coaching.* Paper presented at the annual conference of Consulting Psychology, Phoenix, AZ.

Peterson, R. S., Smith, D. B., Martorana, P. V., & Owens, P. D. (2003). The impact of chief executive officer personality on top management team dynamics. *Journal of Applied Psychology, 88,* 795–808.

Pfeffer, J. (1992). *Managing with power.* Boston: Harvard Business School Press.

Piccolo, R. F., Judge, T. A., & Ilies, R. (2003, April). *The Ohio State Studies: Consideration and initiating structure revisited.* Paper presented at the 17th annual conference of the Society for Industrial and Organizational Psychology, Orlando, FL.

Pocock, T. (1987). *Horatio Nelson.* London: Bodley Head.

Rapoport, A. (1967). Exploiter, leader, hero, and martyr: The four archetypes of the 2x2 game. *Behavioral Science, 12,* 81–84.

Ridgeway, C. L. (1983). *The dynamics of small groups.* New York: St. Martin's.

Riggio, R. E. (1989). *Social skills inventory manual.* Palo Alto, CA: Consulting Psychologists Press.

Roberts, B. W., & Hogan, R. (Eds.). (2001). *Applied personality psychology: The intersection of personality and I/O psychology.* Washington, DC: American Psychological Association.

Roethlisberger, F. J., & Dickson, W. J. (1939). *Management and the worker.* Cambridge, MA: Harvard University Press.

Rousseau, D. M. (1990). Assessing organizational culture. In B. Rowe, D. C. (1997). Genetics, temperament, and personality. In R. Hogan, J. Johnson, & S. Briggs (Eds.), *Handbook of personality psychology* (pp. 369–386). San Diego, CA: Academic.

Ryle, G. (1948). *The concept of mind.* New York: Basic Books.

Salancik, G., & Pfeffer, J. (1977). Constraints on administrator discretion: The limited influence of mayors on city budgets. *Urban Affairs Quarterly, 12,* 475–498.

Sartre, J.-P. (1960). *Critique de la raison dialectique* [Critique of dialectical reasoning]. Paris: Gallimard.

Schmitt, N. (2004). Beyond the Big Five: Increases in understanding and practical utility. *Human Performance, 17,* 347–357.

Schneider, B. (1987). The people make the place. *Personnel Psychology, 40,* 437–453.

Selznick, P. (1957). *Leadership in administration.* New York: Harper & Row.

Sessa, V. I., Kaiser, R. B., Taylor, J. K., & Campbell, R. J. (1998). *Executive selection.* Greensboro, NC: Center for Creative Leadership.

Senior, B. (1997). Team roles and team performance. *Journal of Occupational and Organizational Psychology, 70,* 241–258.

Shaw, M. E. (1976). *Group dynamics.* New York: McGraw-Hill.

Smith, M. L., Glass, G. V., & Miller, T. I. (1980). *The benefits of psychotherapy.* Baltimore: Johns Hopkins University Press.

Stanovich, K. E. (1999). *Who is rational?* Mahwah, NJ: Lawrence Erlbaum Associates.

Steiner, I. D. (1972). *Group process and productivity.* New York: Academic.

Stern, J. M., Shiely, J. S., & Ross, L. (2001). *The EVA challenge: Implementing value-added change in an organization.* New York: Wiley.

Super, D. (1957). *The psychology of careers.* New York: Harper & Row.

Swartz, D. (1997). *Culture and power: The sociology of Pierre Bourdieux.* Chicago: University of Chicago Press.

Taylor, F. (1911). *The principles of scientific management.* New York: 1st World Library.

Thomas, A. (1988). Does leadership make a difference to organizational performance? *Administrative Science Quarterly, 33,* 388–400.

Trist, E. L., & Bamforth, K. W. (1951). Some social and psychological consequences of the long-wall method of coal-getting. *Human Relations, 14,* 3–38.

Tuckman, B. W. (1965). Developmental sequence in small groups. *Psychological Bulletin, 63,* 384–399.

Van Vugt, M., & De Cremer, D. (1999). Leadership in social dilemmas: The effects of group identification on collective actions to provide public goods. *Journal of Personality and Social Psychology, 76,* 587–599.

Van Vugt, M., & Van Lange, P. A. M. (in press). Psychological adaptations for prosocial behavior: The altruism puzzle. In M. Schaller, D. Kenrick, & J. Simpson (Eds.), *Evolution and social psychology.* New York: Psychology Press.

Vosniadou, S., & Brewer, W. F. (1987). Theories of knowledge restructuring in development. *Review of Educational Research, 57,* 51–67.

Vroom, V. H., & Jago, A. G. (1988). *The new leadership.* Englewood Cliffs, NJ: Prentice Hall.

Waldroop, J., & Butler, T. (1998, November 23). Eight failings that bedevil the best. *Fortune, 54,* 27–31.

Warclawski, J., & Church, A. H. (2002). *Organization development.* San Francisco: Jossey-Bass.

Weber, M. (1947). *The theory of social and economic organizations* (A. M. Henderson & T. Parsons, Trans.). New York: Free Press.

Wiggins, J. S. (Ed.). (1996). *The Five-Factor Model of personality.* New York: Guilford.

Wilson, D. S., Near, D., & Miller, R. R. (1996). Machiavellianism: A synthesis of the evolutionary and psychological literatures. *Psychological Bulletin, 119,* 285–299.

Wilson, E. O. (1975). *Sociobiology: The new synthesis.* Cambridge, MA: Harvard University Press.

Wilson, T. D. (2002). *Strangers to ourselves: Discovering the adaptive unconscious.* Cambridge, MA: Harvard University Press.

Yukl, G. (1998). *Leadership in organizations* (4th ed.). Upper Saddle River, NJ: Prentice Hall.

Zaccaro, S. J. (2001). *The nature of executive leadership.* Washington, DC: American Psychological Association.

Zaccaro, S. J. (2002). Organizational leadership and social intelligence. In R. E. Riggio, S. E. Murphy, & F. J. Pirozzolo (Eds.), *Multiple intelligences and leadership* (pp. 29–54). Mahwah, NJ: Lawrence Erlbaum Associates.

Zickar, M. J. (2001). Using personality inventories to identify thugs and agitators: Applied psychology's contribution to the war against labor. *Journal of Vocational Behavior, 59,* 149–164.

Author Index

A

Alexander, R. A., 92
Alliger, G., 36
Allport, G. W., 24
Anderson, J. R., 98
Antonakis, J., 41
Atwater, L., 41
Austin, J. R., 81
Avolio, B. J., 34

B

Bamforth, K. W., 55
Bandura, A., 48
Barrett, L., 45
Barrick, M. R., 63, 92
Barron, F., 19, 20
Barthol, R. P., 51
Bartunek, J. M., 81
Bass, B. M., 43, 49
Belbin, R. M., 65
Bell, B. S., 54, 60, 61, 73
Bentz, V. J., 112, 117
Bernreuter, R. G., 20
Berson, Y., 34
Boehm, C., 3, 34, 39, 40, 43, 45
Bono, J. E., 11, 27, 36, 51
Bourdieu, P., 86
Bowlby, J., 5

Boyatzis, R. A., 46, 112
Brewer, W. F., 135
Browne, J., 8
Bruke, H., 131
Buchanan, J. M., 82
Burke, M. J., 148
Buss, A. H., 23
Butcher, J. N., 20
Butler, T., 109
Byrne, J. A., 103

C

Cairo, P. C., 131
Caldwell, D. F., 72
Campbell, R. J., 37
Cascio, W., 56
Charan, R., 111, 131
Chatman, J., 72
Cherns, A., 55
Church, A. H., 81
Collins, J., 39, 47
Colvin, G., 111, 131
Costa, P. T., Jr., 26
Curphy, G., 35, 74, 143, 146
Cyert, R., 88

D

Dahlstrom, W. G., 20

Dawkins, R., 44
Day, D. V., 92
Day, R. R., 148
De Cremer, D., 43
Degler, C. N., 134
DeHartog, L., 34
Deming, W. E., 56
Denes-Raj, V., 147
DeVader, C. L., 36, 38
DeVries, D. L., 148
Diamond, J., 4, 31, 83
Dickson, W. J., 24, 47, 96
Dirks, K. T., 39
Dixon, N., 47
Dotlich, D. L., 131
Driskell, J. E., 69, 75
Dulewicz, V., 65
Dunbar, R., 45
Durham, D. D., 141
Durkheim, E., 144

E

Emler, N. P., 51
Epstein, S., 147
Erez, A., 11

F

Fernandez-Araoz, C., 106, 108
Ferrin, D. L., 39
Fiedler, F. E., 44
Finn, R. H., 67
Finn, S. E., 149
Fischer, C. T., 149
Fleishman, E. A., 49
Flynn, J. R., 22
Foti, R. J., 38
French, J. R. P., 39, 89
Frenz, H., 88
Funder, D. C., 17, 25, 143

G

Gerhardt, M. W., 27, 36, 51
Ghiselli, E. E., 51
Ghosal, S., 131
Glass, G. V., 149
Goffman, E., 59
Goleman, D., 28

Golembiewski, R. T., 60
Gottier, R. F., 51
Gottlieb, G., 23
Gough, H. G., 20
Graham, J. R., 20
Guion, R. M., 51

H

Hackman, J. R., 55, 60, 61, 67
Hambrick, D. C., 88, 92, 93
Harter, J. K., 38, 92
Hayes, T. L., 38, 92
Haythorn, W. W., 61
Hedlund, J., 62
Heier, H., 148
Henley, N., 90
Herzberg, F., 55, 105
Heuer, H., 136
Hicks, M. D., 134, 138
Hirschey, M., 97
Hogan, J., 14, 16, 19, 35, 36, 43, 62,
        75, 118, 141, 143, 146, 147
Hogan, R., 13, 14, 16, 19, 25, 26, 27,
        29, 35, 36, 43, 45, 52, 58, 62,
        69, 75, 90, 118, 140, 141,
        142, 143, 145, 146, 147
Hogg, M. A., 44
Holland, B. R., 27, 142
Holland, J. L., 67, 95, 99
Hollenbeck, J. R., 62
Hunt, J. G., 41

I

Ilgen, D. R., 62
Ilies, R., 27, 36, 49, 51

J

Jago, A. G., 39
Jenkins, R., 8
Jensen, A., 22
Joyce, W. F., 92
Judge, T. A., 11, 27, 36, 49, 51, 141
Jung, D. I., 34

K

Kaemmer, B., 20
Kahan, J. P., 60
Kahn, R. L., 97

Kaiser, R. B., 37, 48, 49, 50, 51, 143, 145, 148
Kaplan, R. E., 48, 49, 50, 51, 145
Katz, D., 97
Kellerman, B., 40
Kenrick, D. T., 25
Kets de Vries, M. F. R., 95
Klimoski, R. J., 54
Kluger, A. N., 141
Kornhauser, A., vii
Koslowski, S. W. J., 54, 57, 60, 61, 73
Kouzes, J. M., 28, 38, 142

L

Lawler, E. E., 57
Ledford, G. E., Jr., 57
Leonard, H. S., 49
LePine, J. A., 62
Levine, J. M., 61
Locke, E. A., 141
Lombardo, M. M., 106, 113, 114, 117
Lord, R. G., 36, 38, 92
Lycett, J., 45

M

MacIntyre, A. C., 86
Mann, R. D., 60
March, J. G., 89, 96
Marsh, J., 88
Martorana, P. V., 92
Maynard-Smith, J., 44
McAdams, D., 8, 12
McCall, M. W., Jr., 106, 113, 117
McCauley, C. D., 114
McCauley, M. H., 28
McCormick, E. J., 67
McCrae, R. R., 26
McGrath, J. E., 67
Mead, G. H., 142
Milgram, S., 25
Miller, D., 95
Miller, R. R., 44
Miller, T. I., 149
Mintzberg, H., 39
Mischel, W., 14, 25, 51
Mohammed, S., 54
Mohrman, S. A., 57
Moreland, R. L., 61
Morris, C. G., 60, 61, 67

Mumford, M. D., 71
Myers, I. B., 28

N

Near, D., 44
Neubert, M. J., 63
Neuman, G. A., 64
Newell, A., 135
Nicholson, N., 43, 45
Nohria, N., 92

O

Oldham, G. R., 55
Olsen, J., 89, 96
Ones, D. S., 11, 146
O'Reilly, C. A., III, 72
Owens, P. D., 92

P

Pacini, R., 147
Paul, A. M., 19
Peterson, D. B., 134, 138, 149
Peterson, R. S., 92
Pfeffer, J., 89, 92
Piccolo, R. F., 49
Pocock, T., 39
Posner, B. Z., 28, 38, 142

R

Rapoport, A., 44
Raven, B. H., 39, 89
Raza, S., 69
Ridgeway, C. L., 60, 61
Riggio, R. E., 143
Roberson, B., 92
Roberts, B. W., 25, 26
Roethlisberger, F. J., 24, 96
Ross, L., 98
Rousseau, D. M., 72
Rowe, D. C., 23
Ruderman, M. N., 114
Ryle, G., 136

S

Salancik, G., 92
Salas, E., 75
Sartre, J.-P., 86

Scheirs, D. C., 67
Schmidt, F. L., 11, 38, 92, 146
Schmitt, N., 17
Schneider, B., 95
Selznick, P., 81
Sessa, V. I., 37
Senior, B., 65
Shavelson, R. J., 60
Shaw, M. E., 60
Shiely, J. S., 98
Simon, H. A., 96, 135
Smith, D. B., 92
Smith, M. L., 149
Sosik, J. J., 34
Stanovich, K. E., 147
Steiner, I. D., 60, 61
Stern, J. M., 98
Stewart, G. L., 63
Stokes, L. W., 29
Stolzenberg, R. M., 60
Super, D., 72
Swartz, D., 88

T

Taylor, F., 82
Taylor, J. K., 37
Tellegen, A., 20
Terrell, M. E., 98
Thomas, A., 92
Toulouse, J.-M., 95
Trist, E. L., 55
Tuckman, B. W., 73

V

Van Lange, P. A. M., 45
Van Vugt, M., 43, 45
Viswesvaran, C., 11, 146
Vosniadou, S., 135
Vroom, V. H., 39

W

Waldroop, J., 109
Warclawski, J., 81
Warrenfeltz, R. W., 140
Webb, N., 60
Weber, M., 82, 93
Wichern, D., 97
Wiggins, J. S., 9, 26, 59, 61
Wilson, D. S., 44
Wilson, T. D., 14, 43
Wright, J., 64

Y

Yukl, G., 39

Z

Zaccaro, S. J., 41, 148
Zickar, M. J., vii

Subject Index

A

Adaptability, 134-135
Affectivity, 10
Applied psychology, vii, 27, 29
Argumentative persons, 120–121
Arrogant persons, 124–125
Attachment theory, 5

B

Behaviorism, 24–25, 135–136, 147
Bounded rationality, 96
Business strategy, 96, 99

C

California Psychological Inventory
   (CPI), 20
Cautious persons, 121–122
Change, 89, 91, 96, 117, 122, 133–135,
   148–149
Character, 12–13, 108, 131, *see also*
   Personality
Colorful persons, 127–128

D

Diligent persons, 129–130

Domination, 4
Downsizing, 54, 57–58, 104
Dutiful persons, 130–131
Dyads, 53

E

Egalitarian bands, 3
Emler's moral rules, 46–48
Emotional intelligence (EQ), 28–29,
   119, 142
Employee dissatisfaction, 38
Equal Employment Opportunity Com-
   mission (EEOC), 27
Evolutionary game theory, 44–45
Excitable persons, 119

F

FFM, 26–27
Flynn effect, 22

G

Garbage can model, 96–97
Gestalt psychology, 135–137
Groups, 2–4, 33–34, 42, 52–53, 60–61,
   72–73, 78, 83, 88, 92, 94, 97,
   148

management groups, 91–93
social groups, 5, 32, 71
task groups, 71
work groups, 43, 58, 65, 69–70
Group effectiveness, 60–61

H

Hierarchy, 3–5, 34, 43, 47, 82, 85–86,
141
Hogan Development Survey (HDS),
41–42, 118–119
dimensions, 119–131
Hogan Personality Inventory (HPI), 16,
41, 62, 75
Humanistic psychology, 55–56
Human nature, viii–ix, 1–2, 45, 84, 90,
134–135, 139

I

Identity, 8–9, 12, 15, 38, 43, 54, 58–59,
72, 78–79, 144
Imaginative persons, 128–129
Incompetence, *see* Managerial incom-
petence
Industrial/Organizational (I/O) psy-
chology, vii, 27, 51
Inner perspective, 144–145
Interpersonal skills, 141–147
Interpersonal theory, 115–117
Intrapersonal skills, 141–142, 145–147
Intrapsychic tradition, 115

L

Law of nomological
nonbiodegradability, 90
Leadership, vii–viii, 2, 18, 27–29,
31–51, 53, 66, 71, 79, 82,
91–99, 101, 103, 105–106,
109–113, 131, 139–150
and followers, 45–46
binding people, 42–43
characteristics, 35–42
competencies, 48–50
effective leadership, 36, 99, 108
Leadership skills, 98, 112, 133, 141,
145, 148–150
Learning, 11–12, 48, 62, 77, 117,
133–150

and development, 137–138
and motivation, 138–140
resistance, 146–148
Leisurely persons, 123–124

M

Management, vii, 38–41, 54–57, 65, 71,
80–82, 89, 97–112, 125,
132–142, 147
education of, 135–137, 141
skills, 138, 141–144
top management, 88, 92–94
Managerial domain model of education, 140–145
education resistance, 146–148
outcomes, 148–150
skills, 141–144
Managerial failure, 112–115, 131–132
derailment factors, 119–132
Managerial incompetence, 101–105,
107–109
fixing it, 133–140
models of bad management,
109–112
worker demotivators, 105–107
Managers, 2, 27, 32, 38–42, 46–50,
56–58, 65, 70–71, 91–100,
102–117, 127–134, 140–143
bad ones, 38, 42, 98, 100, 105–108,
111, 127, 132
good ones, 42, 71, 114, 142–143
moral competencies, 46–48
performance, 49–50
Mischievous persons, 125–126
MMPI, 20–21
Mood, 10, 105, 115
Moral competencies, 46–48
Motivation, 4–7, 55, 68, 80, 87, 98
and learning, 138–140
factors, 105
Motives, Values, Preferences Inventory
(MVPI), 75
Myers-Briggs Type Indicator (MBTI), 28

N, O

New Age psychology, 23–24
Operational leadership, 49
Organizational effectiveness, 97–100
productivity, 55, 57, 97–98, 109,
127, 130

Organizational culture, 95–96, 72
Organizational performance, 2, 57,
    92–93
Organizational phenomena, ix, 80–81
Organizational theory, 2, 81–86
    structural sociology, 81, 134
Organizations defined, 82
    business organizations, 1–2, 97, 99
    psychological taxation, 94–95
    rules, 90
    social organizations, 31–32, 86
    themes, 84–89
Outer perspective, 144–145

P

Performance perspectives, 144–146
Personality, 8–10, 113
    academic criticism, 22–25
    change, 14–15
    development, 10–12
Personality assessment, 17–28
Personality disorders, 115–119
Personality psychology, 13–23, 80, 86
    in the 1960s, 17, 20, 22
    in the 1990s, 26–30
    setbacks, 18–25
Personality theory, viii
Power, 7, 11, 17, 24, 27, 32, 37, 45–49,
    58, 64, 74, 76, 81, 83, 85–89,
    91, 93, 99, 122, 139–140, 147
Process gridlock, 111
Psychotherapy, 148–149
Pyramid schemes, 85–86
Public lives, 52–53

R

Race, 22–23
Recruitment flaws, 108–109
Religion, 3–6, 31, 86
Reputation, 8–9, 15, 38, 144
Reserved persons, 122–123
Restraint, 10
Role balance, 65–66
Role performance, 58–60

S

Self-actualization, 18–19, 55, 139
Self-advancement, 52, 90
Situational influences, 17
Skills, 138, 141–147
Social interaction, 5–9, 26, 58
Socioanalytic theory, 58
Sociotechnical systems, 54–55
Strategic leadership, 49

T

Tasks, 43, 49, 55, 61–69, 71, 75, 125,
    129–130, 148
Team culture, 72–73
Team effectiveness, 60–65
    Belbin's model, 65
    building effective teams, 65–67,
        73–77, 140, 144
    metatheoretical model, 62
Team performance, 53–54, 62–67,
    73–75, 79
Team phenomena, 80
Team roles, 65–67
Teams, 36, 53, 58–65, 71, 73–78, 80,
    93, 121, 144
    history of, 54–57
    management teams, 93
Team tasks, 67–72
    the Holland model, 70
Temperament, 10, 59
Total Quality Management (TQM),
    56–57
Traits, 17–18, 23
Triads, 53

U

Unconscious, 13–14, 81, 85, 115, 135,
    139, 142
U.S. presidents, 113

V, W

Vocational types, 70
Watson-Gleser Critical Thinking Mea-
    sure, 41
Weltanschaung, 17, 22–25